Soul Stories

October 29, 1996

Dear Pat,

    May God's blessings be yours in abundance as you continue your life story.

                Grace and Peace,
                Anne

Soul Stories

African American
Christian
Education

Anne Streaty Wimberly

Abingdon Press
Nashville

SOUL STORIES
AFRICAN AMERICAN CHRISTIAN EDUCATION

Copyright © 1994 by Abingdon Press

This book is printed on recycled, acid-free paper.

Library of Congress Cataloging-in-Publication Data

Wimberly, Anne Streaty, 1936-
    Soul stories : African American Christian education / Anne Streaty Wimberly.
        p. cm.
    ISBN 0-687-00932-4 (pbk. : alk. paper)
    1. Afro-American Sunday schools. 2. Storytelling in Christian education.
    3. Christian education—Biographical methods. 4. Afro-Americans—Religious life.
I. Title.
BV1523.A37W55   1994
236'.1'0940902—dc20   94-7422
                                                                                       CIP

Scripture quotations, unless otherwise noted, are from the New Revised Standard Version of the Bible, copyright © 1989 by the Division of Christian Education of the National Council of the Churches of Christ in the USA. Used by permission.

Quotations by Howard Thurman are from *The Inward Journey,* © 1961 by Howard Thurman, and *Disciplines of the Spirit,* © 1963 by Howard Thurman. Used by permission of The Howard Thurman Educational Trust.

96 97 98 99 00 01 02 03 — 10 9 8 7 6 5 4 3 2
MANUFACTURED IN THE UNITED STATES OF AMERICA

To
My husband, Edward Powell Wimberly;
My mother, Valeska Bea Streaty;
My father, the late Robert Harold Streaty, Sr.,
whose attentiveness to story
inspired my own process of story-linking

CONTENTS _____

ACKNOWLEDGMENTS _____

I am exceedingly grateful to:

Dr. Rosemary Keller and Dr. Jack Seymour, faculty members of the Garrett-Evangelical Theological Seminary, who gave caring encouragement and skillful guidance in this writing venture.

My students in the course, Christian Education in the Black Church, at the Interdenominational Theological Center, Atlanta, Georgia, during the 1991–92 and 1992–93 academic years, who urged and inspired me to write and graciously responded to the results.

The Sunday school attendees at the Rocky Head United Methodist Church, Atlanta, Georgia, whose willing engagement in the story-linking process gave me motivation, direction, and insight.

The respondents who gave me the privilege of many, many hours of sharing and the gift of their personal stories.

Dr. Grant Shockley, Mrs. Doris Shockley, and Ms. Cecelia Long, for their ongoing encouragement and willingness to serve as readers.

Dr. Allen Mayes, Mrs. LaVerne Mayes, Ms. Vidette Bullock, Mrs. Elina Dorado, The Reverend George Dorado, The Reverend Keith Maxwell, Mrs. Barbara Maxwell, The Reverend Leo Constantino, Mrs. Norma Constantino, The late Mr. Dave Mohr, and Ms. Kathy Baliunas whose abiding love and friendship were remembered and held deep within my heart as I wrote the book.

My family, especially to my husband, Ed, who listened to my ideas, critiqued my writings, typed numerous pages, and gave me continuing love, counsel, encouragement, and moral support; my mother, Valeska Streaty, who with great love and care, shared her thoughts and precious, depthful, and unforgettable moments of story-linking with me; and my sister, Roberta Towell, who somehow always knew when to give the much needed pep talk and supportive words.

FOREWORD _____

Anne Streaty Wimberly summarized her unique and exciting book *Soul Stories* when she described it as the outcome of an African American Christian's search for liberation and vocation. Dr. Wimberly, Associate Professor of Christian Education and Church Music at Atlanta's Interdenominational Theological Center, is an experienced teacher and researcher. She has taught at several colleges and seminaries including Garrett-Evangelical Theological Seminary as an adjunct professor. She has done research as Scholar-in-Residence at the Claremont School of Theology Institute for Religion and Wholeness, now called the Howard Clinebell Institute, as well as for The United Methodist Church General Board of Global Ministries.

From years of teaching across all age-levels and cultures and especially in teaching African Americans, she has developed and reintroduced a "new-yet-old" teaching genre, explicitly helpful in working with black children, youths, and adults in their struggles to experience themselves as whole. This approach links stories and biblical images with the exigencies of everyday black experiencing.

Dr. Wimberly's volume, one of a few book-length publications in the area of teaching African American Christians, has several excellent features. It joins the themes of liberation and Christian vocation in the more ample context of Christian discipleship development. It addresses the issues of the imperative need for liberation education in personal and day-to-day living with the current demand for action in the social arena. It faithfully relates the reconciling message of the Bible through symbol, myth, and story to the persistent human struggle of African Americans. Finally, compellingly and interestingly, it shares the hope of the biblical vision of the "beloved community" as it can be realized through personal spiritual renewal and social reconstruction.

The key that unlocks this volume is its clear and succinct organizational design. Developed for Christian education leaders, teachers, ministers, parents, and various age-level participants, it intentionally seeks to assist African Americans in sensing, identifying, and effectively dealing with varied cries for liberation. The author presents all of this within the framework of a Christian perspective.

Soul Stories: African American Christian Education will engage leaders, teachers, and students in a dialogical process of quest and exploration, linking their stories of everyday struggle with Scripture in such a way that Scripture can guide everyday decision making. The first part of the book explores self and world, life events, and life meanings. The latter half of the book prepares teachers and leaders to actually do storytelling, story-linking, and story interpretation. It also guides them in the use of the Bible and the implementation of effective group procedures for teaching. The genius of this book by a younger Christian educator is its recovery of the story method in teaching, relating it to African American heritage and grounding it in a biblical hermeneutic. The author's careful handling of the story-linking process is more than an efficient methodology for Christians. It indicates a new paradigm.

Grant S. Shockley
Professor Emeritus of Christian Education
The Divinity School of Duke University

PREFACE _____

This book presents a contemporary model of Christian education from an African American perspective. The model draws on Christian education approaches initiated during the slave era. It entails a teaching/learning process focused on liberation and vocation. This model aims to enhance leaders' and teachers' abilities to make choices, while providing a method by which those same leaders and teachers can guide the decision making of their students.

Central to the model is the concept of story-linking. Story linking is a process whereby persons connect components of their everyday life stories with the Christian faith story found in Scripture. Participants also connect their personal stories with Christian faith heritage stories of African Americans found outside Scripture. More specifically, persons link with Bible stories/texts by using them as a mirror through which they reflect critically on the liberation and vocation they have already found or are still seeking. This linkage helps persons to discern the liberating activity of God and God's call to vocation—living in the image of Christ—in both biblical and present times.

In linking with Christian faith heritage stories of African Americans, persons relate themselves to exemplars who chose ways of living in community that were informed by the gospel. The intent is for African Americans to be encouraged and inspired by the lives of persons who faced life circumstances with which they can readily identify. And it is aimed toward persons' choosing to cooperate with this activity by acting in ways that are liberating for them and others.

Five primary assumptions undergird the story-linking model of Christian education presented in the book.

1. Christian education can be strengthened or extended beyond the present paradigm by reclaiming the story-linking process found in the early slave community.

2. The story-linking model is appropriately undertaken in inter-generational Christian education settings.

3. There is similarity between the issues as well as the contexts that are addressed in Scripture and the issues and the contexts African Americans address today.

4. The story-linking model can be used appropriately in traditional Christian education settings such as the church school, Bible study settings, and in combinations of age/stage groups. However, it is also useful in the home and other community settings.

5. The story-linking model holds importance for Christian education leaders, teachers, and participants alike.

Impetus for Writing the Book

This book has emerged out of my recognition that Christian education for African Americans is at a crossroads. On the one hand, its historical role in African American churches is undisputed. Leaders see clearly its potential for providing direction, experiences, and resources that meet current challenges of African Americans. Because of their view of the pivotal role of Christian education, some churches have given specific attention to redesigning or appending traditional programs.

On the other hand, there is much discussion among present and future African American church leaders about the great challenge currently facing Christian education in African American churches and communities. Many churches pay more attention to worship and give less attention to Christian education. In numerous instances, Christian education is a neglected facet of African American church life.

Agreement exists among African American Christian educators and leaders that individuals and families seek greater relevance and effectiveness in Christian educational contexts and processes. People desire a context and a process for exploring, reflecting on, and deciding on ways of living as Christians. There is need for reflection on how we are living as persons in community, the choices we have made, and the purpose we see for our lives in the face of predictable life crises and everyday life experiences.

Persons are searching for forums in which they can address who they are and can become in their everyday social contexts. They also desire guidance in seeing options and deciding, consciously and intentionally, ways of living and serving as Christians that are liberating and that imbue their lives with meaning and purpose. This means that persons are seeking help with the task of ethical decision making. It is out of my recognition of these needs and desires in the contemporary African American church and community that this book is written.

The Soul's Search for Liberation and Vocation

We may not live out all our days
Tensing every nerve to do our best
To find at last a dead goal, a false road.
How may we know?
Is there no guide for us?
No shining light by which our steps are led?
Through all the chaos of our years
We seek to know.

—HOWARD THURMAN
THE INWARD JOURNEY

One of the questions I often ask participants in African American Christian education settings is, "What brought you here?" or "What prompts you to come?" Their answers give me, as the Christian educator, insights into what they seek from their involvement and what they might be receiving. The question also invites participants to consider their own motivations and goals. A typical response is, "No one has ever asked me that question before, but now that you ask . . . ." What invariably results is an enlightening disclosure of personal thoughts of which the following are indicative:

SOUL STORIES

"I go to Sunday school to tap into the richness of the Bible. By doing this, I get spiritually fed and my faith gets renewed and strengthened. I enjoy the study. Really, I'm hungry to find out what is in the Bible. I want to know what God's will is for my life. I want to see what the Bible has to say for what I need to do with my life and how I can face all of the things that come at me every day."

"It is important for me to be able to talk about the problems and the concerns I face every day and to come to some idea about how to handle them. We don't always do this. But, when we do, it helps me. I see attending Sunday school as a time when I can draw strength from what the Bible has to say. I come to find answers to questions I have about what to do. I need to hear the words and the messages that can take me a step beyond where I am. I need to be able to see that I'm going to make it in spite of whatever problems I am facing. This is why I come."

"Sometimes you don't feel free to share the things that are very personal to you. It's not always comfortable enough to do that. I wish that there was a way for us to do more sharing at that level. To me, Sunday school is a place to talk about the things that are important to us and to get help. When we know that others share some of the same problems, we are better able to study together, learn together, and help one another better. I keep coming, though, because there are times when this does happen."

"Being involved in Sunday school and Bible study groups has been freeing for me spiritually and in other ways too. That's what I want. That's what makes me feel good about going. It is not always what the teacher teaches that makes the difference. I get a great deal out of talking to other persons and hearing what others have to say. I can remember a particular time when we shared about persons we knew who were in need. We got into a discussion about what the Bible had to say about Christian responsibility. We talked about what we thought we ought to be doing. This led to our deciding on specific things to do. We made plans and carried them out. Isn't this what it's all about? Developing relationships? Sharing with others? Studying the Bible? Doing for others and knowing why we're doing it? I think so."

"I've gone to Sunday school almost all my life. It seems that it's always been a habit to go to everything the church offers. Over the years, Sunday school has become an important part of my life, though. Right now, I go for the interaction. This allows me to get something different than it's possible to get in church services."

These and other responses have made me keenly aware that African Americans participate in Christian education because they are seeking from it something deeply important. Many participants seek spiritual and educational enrichment through their dialogue with the Bible and one another. They want to gain insights, and they seek to free their imaginations in ways that deepen their spiritual lives and their relationships with others.

Some seek to validate ways they have handled life struggles or how they are now living out the intricate details of their lives. Some look for specific answers to issues and questions arising from dire life circumstances. They seek freedom from these circumstances and pathways to a better and more meaningful life. Others seek insights and guidance that can result in their lives being changed and set in a new direction.

There are occasions, too, when persons are not quite sure why they are in attendance. Initially, someone may have directed them there or they may have accompanied another, or they may say simply that they felt attendance was expected of them. Often persons have more than one reason. Moreover, persons find that the reasons for their involvement are not always the same. They enter Christian education contexts at different junctures in their lives for different reasons. Some drop out and others do not come because they do not find there what they seek.

Reflection Exercise. Consider your own experiences in Christian education. In what settings have you participated? What prompted your involvement? What did you hope would happen in your life as the result of your participation?

19

A Quest for Liberation and Vocation

Whether persons attend church school, Bible study groups, youth groups, or other Christian education settings in church, home, or community, African Americans often tell of a deep inner yearning. This deep inner yearning is their soul's search for liberation and vocation. Globally, their deep inner yearning for liberation is their desire to experience themselves as whole or moving toward wholeness. They want to move beyond external and internal barriers that block their experiences of positive relationships with God, self, others, and all things. They seek guidance in doing this from a Christian perspective. Their deep yearning for vocation is their desire to see and to act on their value and purpose in the world as human beings who are Christian. They seek help in satisfying this desire from a Christian vocational standpoint.

African American leaders and teachers, too, bring to the Christian education context their life stories and an inner quest for ongoing liberation and vocation. They seek release from bonds not unlike those of the participants. As one teacher put it, "Sometimes I feel so burdened down, that it is hard for me to feel that I have anything to give to my students. I face problems as great as theirs and I am searching, too, for a way through them."

Christian education leaders and teachers also seek purpose and meaning in life. For some, leadership in Christian education is, in part, a way of honoring their liberation and vocational quest. When asked why she became a Sunday school teacher, for example, a teacher replied, "Teaching gives me an opportunity to give back to God and to the church what they have done for me. I want to be able to contribute something to somebody else's life." Sometimes, teachers' quests for liberation and vocation include desires to break out of their bondage to teaching approaches that have questionable relevance in their contexts.

Teachers seek options that can free their own creative imagination, so that they may free the creative imaginations of the participants. As one youth group leader said, "I know there must be some other way to do things in order to make it exciting and helpful for my youths. But I'm stuck. I'm really in a predicament. I know that for my youths' sake, and for my sake, I've got to get out of this predicament."

In an important way, then, teachers function in a dual role in the liberation and vocational quest. On the one hand, they have specific responsibility for guiding emancipatory teaching and learning processes. On the other hand, teachers are themselves learners who seek emancipatory experiences that can bring about their own ongoing liberation and life meaning and purpose. Their roles as learners make them sharers with the participants in the liberation and vocational quest. As learners, they become mutual sojourners with the participants.

Reflection Exercise. Consider your experiences as a leader or teacher in Christian education. What prompted your involvement as a leader or teacher? What did you hope would happen in your life as the result of your leadership and interaction with participants? What did you hope would happen in the lives of the participants as the result of your leadership?

An Invitation to Story-Linking

The purpose of this book is to engage you in a process that is aimed toward liberation and vocation from a Christian perspective. You have already been invited to respond to some questions. You will be engaged further through a model of Christian education that takes seriously the lived stories of African Americans. Central to the model is a story-linking approach.

The story-linking approach will invite your reflection on positive and problematic contemporary stories. Particularly, you will be invited to consider how liberation and vocation are exhibited in the stories and how liberation and vocation are inhibited. You will also be challenged to identify options and make decisions that create for you the potential for new and ongoing experiences of liberation and vocation in community. To assist you in this process, you will be invited to link your story with the Christian story found in Scripture and with African American Christian faith heritage stories.

This book invites you as Christian education leaders and teachers to engage in story-linking aimed toward your own liberation and vocation. At the same time, it prepares you to invite others into the process with you and to guide them through the process. Whether we are leaders/teachers or participants, all of us are invited to be ongoing learners and mutual sojourners.

Meanings of Liberation and Vocation

When I have invited participants to share their understandings of liberation and vocation, I have discovered that they have important insights formed from inside their experiences. The presence of these "views from the inside" underscore the importance of acknowledging the very real reflective activity in which participants are already engaged. It suggests that persons' liberation and enactment of vocation begin with them. Moreover, the guidance leaders/ teachers give to participants in story-linking processes aimed toward liberation and vocation should build on the participants' prior reflection processes.

A View of Liberation from the Inside

When we ask African American participants in Christian education what it means to be liberated, we are not likely to get one answer. This tendency is revealed in the following statement of an African American male:

"When I think about liberation, what comes to my mind, first, is a feeling of being all right inside myself. I feel like it's okay to be me because I count in God's eyes. I can also be myself, because I know I'm all right as a person, and I'm respected for who I am. But, then, sometimes other folk don't think I'm all right. It seems like they don't want to let me go on with my life in the same way they are allowed to. That's when me and God have to talk, 'cause the way I think God sees me and the way others do are just not the same. You know what I mean?

"Like, on my job, I feel like I can't advance because of who I am as a black man. The attitudes they show toward me as a black man aren't that good either. That's wrong. Well, because I can't seem to advance, I can't get for me and my family all the things we really need. There are times when we see our way clear and we get caught up with things like medical bills and clothes for the kids.

"Well, about liberation? I know what it's not. And, I know that sometimes you see it, sometimes you don't. I know my children see what's going on. I wonder sometimes what it is doing to them. But I do the best I can, and me and my wife keep on trying to encourage our children. We keep our hopes up. So far they're doing well, where some other kids aren't. You know what no hope can do. Whenever I can, I try to do whatever I can for the kids in the neighborhood. People don't always think that black men care, but I do. No, I don't have all the answers for them or for me. I can use some help. Like I said, I do the best I can, but sometimes I know that's not good enough.

"All in all, I'm blessed in so many ways. I was able to get an education. Now, I didn't get to go to college, but I did get vocational technical training, and I took opportunities that came my way to upgrade my skills. That's a part of being liberated too. I want more for my children. Sure, it can be hard to get an education. But then you have to want to get it, and it helps when somebody's there to encourage you. It is something that, when you get it, nobody can take it away from you.

"Well, let me say one more thing. At one time in my life I know I wasn't going in the right direction. I wasn't spiritually right or mentally right and I guess you might say any other kind of right. Things have changed as far as that's concerned. Somewhere along the line, I got a whole new lease on life. I feel like it was the power of God that helped me to turn my life around. I feel all right in my soul, and I try to do what's right by others. To me, that's liberation too. Then, too, my family is my pride and joy. There's nobody that keeps us from loving one another. Then too, there's nobody that keeps us from helping others that aren't close family. Like education, nobody can take that away either. And isn't that what being a Christian is all about? Liberation? There's so many things to it. It's not just one thing."

For this man and other participants with whom I have dialogued, liberation is not a singular or one-time accomplishment. Rather, it appears to be a multidimensional process that doesn't stop. Moreover, the various facets are intricately interwoven. That is, persons themselves assign causal relationships to the various facets of liberation. They will say, for example, that they cannot be liberated in this way because they are not free in that way.

From what African Americans have to say about liberation, it is also clear that one dimension of liberation or another is attained at points in their lives while other dimensions remain elusive. Some dimensions are maintained over long periods while others seem to be short-lived. Persons with whom I have dialogued have identified at least eight dimensions of liberation.

Dimension One. The first dimension involves knowing one's life as gift and oneself as a valued human being rather than being shackled by how society or anyone else sees you. From the Christian viewpoint, one sees oneself as created by God and valued by God. One sees one's identity in God. This may be referred to as liberation from self-denigration to positive self-valuing or positive self-regard. This kind of liberation is shown in the story of the man who said he is liberated because he feels all right inside and okay in being who he is.

Dimension Two. To be liberated is to have the wherewithal by which to receive and maintain, at minimum, the basic necessities of life. From the Christian perspective, this means assuring that all God's children have what is necessary to survive with human dignity and respect. This is liberation from material need to material sustenance. In the man's story, note this liberation was elusive for him. He felt there were blocks to attaining what was fully needed for this to occur.

Dimension Three. A third dimension of liberation is closely aligned to the second one. It is to be equal participants and beneficiaries in the political, occupational, educational, residential, health care, and civic systems of the community and the nation. For Christians, this means assuring the necessities of every member of God's household through granting persons' full participation in life activities leading to their provision. This is liberation from human disenfranchisement to human enfranchisement.

Dimension Four. Liberation requires that persons experience respectful and just treatment by others, including family, friends, and others with whom they have daily contact. From the Christian perspective, this means seeking to destroy whatever blocks the human realization of the value God places on us. We may refer to this activity as liberation from denigration and dehumanization to positive human valuing or positive regard from others. The man in the story was ill-treated at work, but he received love at home.

Dimension Five. Liberated people can see possibilities of breaking out of narrow boundaries of thoughts, knowledge, feelings, and limited beliefs in the self's ability to act. This is liberation from miseducation, no education, and no vision. It is liberation to active learning and arriving at a vision for living. For Christians, it entails active engagement in Christian teaching and learning and arriving at a vision of one's life as Christian. Note in the man's story that he saw ways of doing what he could in the best way he could in spite of adversity. He encouraged his children and maintained hope, and he believed that encouragement, hope, and doing his best made a difference.

Dimension Six. Liberated people recognize their need to share themselves and their stories with another. They also recognize their need to receive the same from others. From the Christian perspective, they see life as a gift worthy of sharing. In the man's statement above, there was shared love in the family. He also said that he tried to do right by others. This is liberation through significant relationship.

Dimension Seven. Liberation results when persons have been changed by God and allow the story of God and the good news of Jesus Christ to direct their lives. They see the difference between living that didn't work for them and life in positive relation to God, self, others, and all things. This is liberation through religious transformation. The African American man quoted earlier does not engage in a great deal of God-talk. However, he is clear that it was by the power of God that his life was turned in the right direction. After this point, he resolved to live the right way by doing right by others.

Dimension Eight. Finally, persons are never fully liberated until they become aware of others' needs for liberation and accept as obligatory their responsibility for contributing to the liberation of others. This dimension of liberation entails mutual caring or the movement away from concerns and actions aimed only toward the self to concerns and actions with and on behalf of others in the way Jesus did. The African American man spoke of his concern for the neighborhood children, of his family as his pride and joy, and of his concern for his children's education. He was aware of their needs for liberation and sought to provide for them in a way that they could experience it.

We need to be aware, however, that just as people express what liberation means, they also have perceptions and experiences of what it means to fall short of it. The African American man's experience and perception of "falling short" prompted his statement that he did not have all the answers. Thus, the quest for liberation and the need for direction in finding pathways to it continued.

Reflection Exercise. You and participants in your Christian education context may see yourselves in the man's story. Or your story may differ from his. How is your story like or different from his? Your views of liberation may also be similar or dissimilar to the various dimensions of liberation outlined above. In what ways have you experienced the dimensions of liberation outlined above? What blocks to the various aspects of liberation have you experienced?

A View of Vocation from the Inside

Vocation is not unrelated to liberation. When we see a purpose for our lives that is related to caring for and helping others, we are liberated to be in vocation. Yet, we often have constricted views of what vocation means for Christians. In a discussion about vocation in a church school class, a participant said, "Vocation is what you do for others, whether you get paid for it or not. It can be related to your occupation, but it doesn't have to be. But the main thing is that you do it because God called you to do it." Another class member confirmed that, "as Christians, we know within ourselves that God wants us to carry out our lives in a way that we and others are built up."

The participants highlighted the central idea of vocation as calling. They also said that for some of them, an initial impression of a direction toward a specific vocation came at an early time in their lives. But they did not fully understand it as God's call. Even when God's call is fully comprehended, persons sometimes say no to it either because they don't perceive it as possible or because of other internal or external blocks. Other participants became aware of their call to vocation when they were "pressed into" a particular helping role or when someone else identified gifts they had that could be used to benefit the community. Still others said that they saw from the lives of others and in their own lives that one's call to vocation can change at different points in their lives. They raised the question about whether vocation is just for the young. One participant exclaimed:

> "If vocation is what you do for others whether you get paid for it or not, then age doesn't matter. Take, for example, volunteering. That can be done at any age. Take, for example, my elderly neighbor. She is raising one of her grandchildren. She is giving that child a stable home that isn't possible with the parents. I'd say she's in vocation, and she's certainly not getting paid for it, not that she shouldn't get paid."

At the same time, African Americans are very aware that when they are called to occupation-related vocations, there is need for preparation and that is where their calling can be blocked. Consider the following story:

> "I always wanted to be somebody and do something important with my life. I'm not sure where I got the idea, but I wanted to be a doctor. When I was a kid, I used to dream about it. I used to ask for a play doctor's bag for Christmas. The only thing was, whenever I said anything about it, I was laughed at. I was told, 'How do you think you're going to do that? Don't you know you're black, boy? There's nobody out there who wants you to get anywhere, and who's going to see that you get anywhere?' They would say, 'Just look where we live. People have a hard time

leaving this place.' You see, we lived in the projects. The teachers in school also treated us as though we weren't supposed to go anywhere either. Somewhere along the line, I stopped believing in me and my dream. That dream got shattered.

"Well, I didn't become the doctor I wanted to be, although I have a good friend who grew up in my neighborhood who beat the odds and did become one. I had some bad times and got into some trouble along the way. But there was somebody looking after me. I guess you'd say I had an angel watching after me. I was able to put my life together, and I am doing something important with my life. I did get through high school. I got involved in a church through a man who witnessed to me about God on a job I took after graduation. I guess you'd call it a miracle.

"It took me awhile. but I decided I wanted to help other kids get out of where somebody told me I couldn't. God helped me to see that I had to do this. I guess you'd say God called me. And, when I realized I had to do something like this, I kept on 'til I found a way of doing it. Now, I am directing a community youth program, and I am going to college to become a guidance counselor. I'm in a place where I can tell the youth that they can go beyond the limits others set for us and that God wants that for us. I just hope I can help them see that and can help move some stumbling blocks along the way."

This African American had an early sense of life direction. But, he did not have the opportunity to discover whether this impression was a definitive call from God. Because he bought into the limits set by others, his response to it was stifled. His liberation to pursue the occupation-focused vocation of physician was blocked by negative regard from others and negative self-regard. However, the young man later received a definitive call from God and responded to it. He identified it as coming through God's help. He recognized it as God's call to him. Another person was also instrumental in his liberation to vocation. Through this person, he saw himself as an instrument in others' liberation. This young man's story is typical of many other stories. But there are cases where the outcome was not as promising. Instead of constructive vocation, persons felt "beaten down" and moved in the direction of destructive behavior.

The young man in the story pinpointed the desire of every African American. He spoke of the desire to be somebody and to do something important in life. In Christian education settings where other African Americans and I have engaged in dialogue about vocation, they have clearly conveyed that everyone, no matter what age, likes to feel that their life counts for something. They understood vocation as the way for this to happen. Thus, for them, vocation is related to forming meaning and purpose or positive worthiness in life. They also clearly convey that, when blocks prevent this from happening, we as African Americans must leave no stone unturned to dismantle them. Their viewpoint is that we must envision, develop, and utilize resources that are in our culture to confront blocks to both liberation and vocation. As one Christian education participant put it:

> "We know from the Bible that it's possible to make it in hard trials, and that's what much of life is. We also know that our African American foreparents made it. We seem to forget that. We need to remember. We need to build strength from the resources from the past and know that the resources here in the present are looking right at us. We just have to see them."

For African Americans, this envisioning, developing, and utilizing resources, past and present, is what may be termed "an overarching cultural vocation."

Not every person comes to Christian education with notions of what the word *vocation* means. Often, it is in dialogue and storytelling that its meaning for them takes shape. Moreover, they may only begin to personalize its meaning when helpful questions are asked, such as:

What are you doing with your life as a Christian?
What is God calling you to be and do?
What meaning and purpose do you assign to your life as a Christian?

Questions such as these tend to open a new window of thought and to give persons an opportunity to voice their experiences and their perceptions of vocation.

I also have found that persons develop understandings of Christian vocation when they see how it is carried out in Bible stories and everyday life. They learn about Christian vocation from what they see and hear from Christian exemplars. Particularly the young want to know how and why adults got involved in what they are doing and what it means to them. This is because African American youths often have a difficult time making sense out of life. They question God. They struggle with their identities, their social contexts, their relationships, and the things that happen to them. They want and need encouragement, affirmation, and support in their quest for positive life meaning and purpose.

African American adults, as well, observe the lives of persons around them and go through questioning similar to our youths. They, too, need encouragement, affirmation, and support. Both want and need opportunities to consider what is going on in their lives, to affirm the positives, and to find how to address precisely the negatives.

In short, African Americans come to Christian education with various understandings of vocation. But regardless of their understandings, they see an important connection between liberation and vocation. They articulate it in their own ways, and they desire guidance in seeing its meaning for their lives.

Reflection Exercise. What are your views of Christian vocation? In what ways are you now fulfilling your Christian vocation or do you intend to fulfill it? If you were to ask participants in your Christian education context what they understand their Christian vocation to be, what would they say? If you were to ask them to share how they are now fulfilling their Christian vocation or intend to fulfill it, what do you think they would say?

Liberation, Vocation, the Everyday Lived Story, and the Christian Story

Whatever our views of liberation or vocation, it is important to be aware that all of us look upon our own liberation and vocation (as well as blocks to them) from inside the stories we live every day. That is, how we view our own liberation and vocation is impacted by every facet of our lives—our self-identities, the social contexts in which we carry out our lives (home, school, work, church, community), relationships in which we are engaged, the life events or incidents that happen to us, and the meanings we assign to life. We may consider one or more of these facets as facilitating our experience of liberation and enactment of vocation. Or, we may consider one or more of them as blocks or deterrents to liberation and vocation.

The story excerpts revealed earlier give us some indication of how liberation, vocation, and the everyday stories of people are connected integrally. By disclosing and reflecting on our stories, we begin the process of seeing ways in which we have experienced liberation and ways in which we have engaged in vocation. We also begin to see ways in which both liberation and vocation have been hindered. This is the first step toward reaching the fullest experience of liberation and vocation.

Still greater insights come when we look at liberation, vocation, and our everyday lived stories in light of the Christian faith story. Often, however, Christian education contexts and processes do not help persons to connect openly their everyday stories with Bible stories/texts. Often, their everyday stories go undisclosed and they remain silent about their need for guidance in their liberation and vocation quest.

The Challenge to Respond to the Soul's Yearning for Liberation and Vocation

Christian educators in African American settings are challenged to provide a Christian education for liberation and vocation. This involves both the *content* or basic meanings of liberation and vocation from an African American Christian perspective and a culturally sensitive *process.* The basic content builds upon the expressions of liberation and vocation from personal experiences such as those related earlier in this chapter. It is rooted in the desire of African Americans for wholeness, their hunger to move beyond external and internal barriers that block their experiences of positive relationships with God, self, others, and all things. I also understand the basic content to be built on the understanding of vocation as African

Americans' desires to see and act on their value and purpose in the world as human beings who are Christian.

A culturally sensitive process will enable persons to break the silences into which they have often been relegated. The challenge is to give them voice, so that they can share their stories, their deepest concerns, and hopes. This is particularly important since African Americans often experience themselves as existing in a culture of the unheard.

Envisioning the Process

A vital Christian education for liberation and vocation is one that offers a process that has at its center our lived stories. That is, the starting point of Christian education for liberation and vocation should be the everyday life stories we face. Such a process should make possible our arriving at insights, discerning choices, and making ethical decisions—decisions about what is right to do to promote and sustain liberation for us and others. The process should also enable us to arrive at insights, discern choices, and make the kinds of ethical decisions that lead to our involvement in vocation from a Christian standpoint.

A process that enables these actions is one that links us to the story of God and the Good News of Jesus Christ reflected in Scripture. A vital Christian education must be forthright in asking the questions, What is it that the Christian story in Scripture has to offer? How may Scripture inform our choices and decisions as African Americans about what is right to do to bring about liberation and the enactment of authentic Christian vocation? To address these questions is to respond to our deepest needs for God's presence and direction in our liberation and vocational quest. By choosing and entering Bible stories/texts that reveal the hardships and sufferings of an earlier people and God's activity in the midst of anguish, we are enabled to envision God's presence and activity now. We are enabled to envision ourselves, as did those in earlier times, in an unfolding story that is undertaken on faith and in faithful cooperation with God's direction.

The intent of Christian education for liberation and vocation is to place us in touch with our African American forebears' faith and their experience of God's action in their liberation and vocation. Linking with our forebears' story helps to inspire us and to foster our commitment to continue on the Christian faith walk. This linkage also promotes our openness and expectation to be continually formed and informed by the story of God and the Good News of Jesus Christ.

Of particular importance are exemplars from the African American heritage who struggled with and overcame tremendous blocks to liberation and who engaged in the kind of ethical decision making that led them into vocation. Of particular importance are predecessors who interpreted and acted on difficult and oppressive life issues by identifying with stories/texts found in Scripture. Our intent is to see as applicable to ourselves what it meant for them to place their lives in dialogue with Bible stories/texts. We want to see how they made a connection between life hoped for and life valuable enough to continue striving for and what this means for us today.

The Importance of Compassionate Listening

We dare not envision Christian education processes without giving serious thought to the quality of settings in which the processes are to occur. It is not enough to say simply that we will do this or that. The emotional environment will have much to do with the success or failure of whatever we attempt to do.

It is my position that we need to do more to make African American Christian education settings nurturing spaces. We need to ensure spaces wherein persons are given voice and can enter into dialogue together in open, caring, and supportive ways. It is important to create spaces where intergenerational dialogue can take place and where socioeconomic differences are transcended. This is an important approach to fulfilling a vision of community where all are considered mutual sojourners.

If we are to be truly emancipatory and focused on Christian vocation, then we must be intentional in our embodiment of the Christian story in the Christian education settings we fashion. This embodiment can happen only as we begin to envision what it means to express *agape love*. This is love that dares to hear others, to enter into the experiences of others, to feel with others their concerns and sufferings, and to envision and anticipate with others ways of confronting their concerns and sufferings. To do this is to engage in "inliving" or living in solidarity with others.[1] This deeply felt sense of solidarity makes it possible for persons to be sustained in their search for liberation and vocation.

Embodying the Christian story through inliving must also include compassionate listening. When we listen compassionately, we show a genuine interest in the concerns and the sufferings of others. As a listening presence, we are also called to be sensitive to the difficulty persons often have in disclosing and confronting life struggles. Compassionate listening is part of creating an environment in which persons feel comfortable to share. When persons feel comfortable enough to share and are encouraged to speak, their stories expose the self. In compassionate listening, the sharings of the self are regarded as gifts and are received with great caring and sensitivity.

In short, an important task of African American Christian educators is to ensure an environment that contains the emancipatory qualities that can foster persons' liberation and enactment of Christian vocation outside that setting.

Reflection Exercise. Consider the quality of your Christian education context. In what ways is it a nurturing space? In what ways are *agape love* and inliving expressed? What areas in the quality of your context need improvement?

A Story-Linking Process

The roots of trees spread out in many directions—seeking always seeking the ground of existence for themselves. . . . They [are] on the hunt—for life.

—*HOWARD THURMAN*
DISCIPLINES OF THE SPIRIT

A friend of mine shared with me a particularly exciting Sunday school class he had recently attended. He said that something had happened that "got the whole class talking in a way they had not done in a long time." He described the lesson as follows:

"After the opening song and prayer, the day's topic entitled 'The Gift' was announced. Immediately after this, one of the class members said he had something to share. It was the story of an incident that had happened to John (not his real name) during the week. The incident had such an impact on him that he said he could not keep the story to himself.

"John was in a car accident. He had somehow gotten preoccupied while he was driving and had rear-ended another car. There were slight damages to the car ahead and to his own. He felt sure that he would have to take responsibility for the repairs because of the type of insurance he had. In talking with the other motorist,

John found himself blurting out his disgust for his attention lapse. He told the other motorist that he had been preoccupied by his wife's illness and said that he was already faced with juggling finances. He said that the accident couldn't have happened at a worse time. Christmas was also coming, and he was concerned about disappointing his children. However, he told the other motorist that he would definitely take care of the damages and that he did not have a habit of foreclosing on his commitments.

"The man and the other motorist then exchanged names and telephone numbers and went on their way. Later that evening, John received a phone call. It was the other motorist who called. The motorist said that he couldn't get out of his mind the troubled look on John's face. The motorist shared with John that he could tell that he was a man of character. The motorist also said, 'And it is Christmas time, isn't it?'

"John told of being 'floored' by what happened next. The motorist told him not to worry about the repairs to his car and that he would have no problems handling them himself. The motorist's last words were, 'I hope your wife gets better. Merry Christmas!'

"As soon as John finished telling his story, another class member said, 'And what do you plan to do for someone else?' John replied, 'You know, I hadn't thought about that. I'll have to give it some thought.'

"The teacher then went on with the lesson, which came from Scripture accounts of Christ's coming. The class was not content to stay strictly with the lesson book as they typically do. They tied John's story to the gift of the coming Christ child told in the Scripture. They talked about the problems that accompanied but did not thwart the Christ child's coming. Different class members told of some of their own times of struggle—times when they thought things wouldn't work out, but finally they did.

"The class wrestled with the class leader's questions, 'What if the motorist hadn't freed John from his obligation to pay for the car damages? What do you do while you're waiting and hoping for a problem to work out, and you're not sure it's going to happen?' The class keyed in on the word, *hope*. They saw this word as the centerpiece in the scripture passage on Christ's coming, and that is what they said they hold on to in hard times. "The class saw John's gift from the motorist, the gift of the Christ child, and hope, as gift all in one. The class viewed the star as the sign of hope. They agreed that, in life, there are times when it is hard to see any hope, but then it seems that out of nowhere a sign of hope appears. One person said that you have to be ready to see hope, though, and let it guide you something like the star guided the shepherds and the wisemen.

"Someone else reminded the class that, as tough as things were for our African American foreparents, they kept hoping and singing about their hoping and keeping on because they hoped; and they kept their hope trained on Jesus whom they knew was with them. The class agreed that we as African Americans today need to do the same, and find out ways and keep trying to make our hopes a reality.

"One class member then said, 'Don't forget the question John was asked after he told his story. It may have something to do with making hope a reality. Remember, he had something to think about?' Another class member replied, 'Don't we all?' They said that when we're given a gift, whether it's a gift like John got or the gift of Christ in our lives or the gift of hope, we are to keep that gift going by our giving to others. The class members then talked for a time about what they as Christians ought to be doing. They gave some examples of people they knew whose lives seemed to be a continuous struggle but who always seem to have a good word for others and who always seem to reach out and give a helping hand. The class also told John that they are available to him and his family to help in any way they could. John said he had something definite in mind that he was going to commit himself to doing for some people he knew that were in worse difficulty then he. Other class members shared similar commitments. The class ended with the singing of the spiritual, 'Rise Up, Shepherd, and Follow.' "

I was particularly struck by this account of a Sunday school lesson because it demonstrates a process of story-linking commonly undertaken by African Americans. In the account, note that John's story about a gift he received became linked with the Bible story about the gift of the Christ child. The class entered the Bible story. From the center of the story, class members reflected critically on their own life stories. The core meaning of the Bible story, which was hope, became their own. They also linked with the story of their African American foreparents. They saw in their story a liberating theme. Or, we might say the foreparents' story revealed a liberation mind-set.

The "call" to John to give to others also became linked to the Scripture and to stories of exemplars of the Christian faith who showed the meaning of vocation in the midst of hard times. This dimension of story-linking brought about additional critical reflection. The process of story-linking ended with the class's focus on decision and action and their use of culturally vital music that revealed, in capsule form, the meaning of the lesson.

Although story-linking has been historically a commonly used process, it is not always incorporated to any great extent in contemporary African American Christian education contexts. The intent here will be to give some direction on how it may be included in these contexts. Attention will be given to the importance of a storied process in Christian education, a definition of story-linking, and a proposed process for story-linking.

Importance of a Storied Process

Throughout every generation, stories reveal the very lives persons live and the lives for which they hope. Stories reveal persons' yearning for God's liberating presence and activity in their lives. And they reveal persons' yearning for meaning and purpose in life. Stories also reveal God's concrete presence and action in persons' lives and persons' responses to God. This is why the story of John in the Sunday school class became the center of discussion. Christian education should be rightly understood as a storied process.

In Christian education from an African American perspective, three primary stories are integral parts of this process: (1) the stories of our everyday lives, (2) the story of God and the Good News of Jesus Christ in Scripture, and (3) postbiblical Christian faith heritage stories, particularly those from the African American Christian faith heritage.

The task is to engage African Americans in story-linking in ways that help us reflect critically on our particular life stories in light of the Christian faith story. A second task is to guide us as African Americans toward envisioning and deciding actions that hold promise for our liberation and vocation in the midst of our particular life situations.

A Definition of Story-Linking

Story-linking is a process whereby we connect parts of our everyday stories with the Christian faith story in the Bible and the lives of exemplars of the Christian faith outside the Bible. In this process, we link with Bible stories by using them as mirrors through which we reflect critically on the liberation we have already found or are still seeking. We also link with our Christian faith heritage by learning about exemplars who chose a way of living based on their understanding of liberation and vocation found in Scripture. By linking with Christian faith heritage stories, we may be encouraged and inspired by predecessors who have faced life circumstances with which we readily identify.

The story-linking process can help us open ourselves to God's call to act in ways that are liberating for us and others and to decide how we will do this. It can also help us discern our vocation, formed and informed by the Christian story, as well as ways of accomplishing it.

A Proposed Process for Story-Linking

Story-linking is comprised of four primary phases: (1) engaging the everyday story, (2) engaging the Christian faith story in the Bible, (3) engaging Christian faith stories from the African American heritage, and (4) engaging in Christian ethical decision making. Each one of the four phases will be discussed in more detail in the following sections.

PHASE ONE: *Engaging the Everyday Story*

We either consciously or unconsciously use our own personal stories as a lens through which we view what is being focused on in Christian education. We interpret the Bible, struggle with its meaning, and respond to God's Word contained in it in light of the realities and demands of our everyday lives. We look at our lives in comparison to the lives of our predecessors and to the ways they lived the Christian story. By placing our stories up front, the intention is not to compromise the importance of the Christian faith story disclosed in the Bible. Rather, the intent is to acknowledge that Christian education leaders/teachers and participants already have an agenda when they come to Christian education. Our stories are the agenda we bring to our study of the Christian faith story in the Bible and our Christian faith heritage story. It is important to disclose this agenda in order that we might intentionally allow our stories to be formed and informed by the Christian faith story.

We may rightly ask, On what should the disclosure of everyday life stories of African Americans focus? In the Sunday school lesson described at the beginning of the chapter, John focuses on a particular life event. But, life events are by no means all that make up our everyday life stories. There are a number of key components of our lives that give shape to our everyday stories. I am proposing six broad interrelated factors that contribute to our stories and that can have either facilitating or inhibiting effects on our liberation and vocation. Each of the six are described below. As you read each description, consider briefly your own story.

Self-Identity

Our stories are shaped by who we perceive ourselves to be as we continue to relate with the world around us. This includes our cultural identity that becomes ours at birth and about which we form perceptions as we go about our lives in our ethnic cultural context and the larger social context. Our self-identity is how we answer the question, Who am I?

Social Contexts

Our stories are shaped by the social contexts in which we live and engage in the affairs of life. Where we live, work, and attend school and church, what these places look and feel like, and what larger society feels like are all parts of the social contexts that help to shape our stories. The quality of our social contexts is informed by the availability or nonavailability of needed resources, as well as kinds and extent of opportunities to participate in them.

Our social contexts are also related to our self-identity. We see ourselves in certain ways in accordance with the qualities comprising our social contexts. We perceive ourselves as like or different from others on the basis of our social contexts. We may also feel ourselves valued or devalued by others on the basis of the social contexts in which we live out our lives.

Interpersonal Relationships

Our stories are shaped by our past and present relationships with persons. These relationships take place in the various social contexts mentioned above. We relate to family members and friends in home and community. We relate to others in church, school, community, and the workplace. We relate to people who are distantly known to us in the political realm and in public media. As Christians, we relate to God through Jesus Christ.

Life Events

Our stories are informed by life events taking place in our social contexts and emerging out of our relationships that remain vivid in our memories. Life events are positive and negative incidents that happen to us over our lives' courses. They include incidents that we celebrate, crises, and other kinds of incidents that cause concern, hardship, or suffering.

Life Meanings

Our stories are informed by the meanings we assign to our lives. Our meaning-making is, in fact, our way of making sense out of our lives through judgments we make about every aspect of our lives. Our meaning-making includes both our thoughts and our feelings about our lives. It includes positive and negative thoughts and feelings about our value and dignity as human beings. In meaning-making, we also ponder the source of our positive or negative valuing of our selves. It also includes what we consider to be the purpose of our lives and what we think and feel about that purpose.

Our Unfolding Story Plot

We approach life and act on life according to the meanings we assign to all of the above components of our lives. In addition, how we choose to act contributes to how every part of our lives unfolds. This makes up our unfolding story plot. We may see life optimistically and approach it in positive and constructive ways or we may see life in negative terms and approach it in destructive ways. How we see life becomes the undergirding theme in our lives and strongly infuences how we act. This gives unique character to our unfolding plot.

In the story-linking process in an actual Christian education context, the entry point can be any one of the aforementioned factors that inform the everyday stories of African Americans. Or no more than two factors may be combined. I have found helpful combining self-identity with life contexts, interpersonal relationships with life events, and life meanings with unfolding story plots.

In focusing on the paired factors, our intent is to consider critically where liberation and vocation are facilitated and where they are blocked. Moreover, the intent is to determine what kinds of decisions are needed to unblock and sustain liberation and vocation.

Because the participants in our Christian education contexts may not have had frequent invitation to self-disclosure, they may need to be assured of their right to choose or not to choose to share. In the actual process of story-linking, there also may be persons who do not feel comfortable sharing the details of their stories or who are, in the beginning, reluctant to do so. To ensure the maximum engagement of participants, a case study method is helpful. Through this method, a preconstructed everyday story is presented that focuses on a particular factor in everyday life. The first phase of the story-linking process evolves from the segment of the case that is presented. Upcoming chapters will illustrate how case material may be used.

As groups become increasingly comfortable with the process and begin to adopt the process as their own, they may provide their own firsthand experiences as the basis for story-linking. However, use of case studies at the outset helps free persons to see and talk about themselves through someone else's story. Through case studies, it is possible for persons to see in their own lives and the lives of group members valuable insights that can be beneficial to their liberation and vocational quests. But, to facilitate this, it is important that leaders/teachers assure free-flowing and open group sharing. This means actively discouraging any expression or contribution that comes across as a put-down.

Three activities comprise phase one. They include the everyday story disclosure, the group's critical reflection on the story, and discussion about how group members identify with the story.

PHASE TWO: *Engaging the Christian Faith Story in the Bible*

In phase two of the story-linking process, the case study material is linked with the story of God and the Good News of Jesus Christ found in Scripture. Recall in the Sunday school lesson summarized early in this chapter that John and the class looked at the Bible story of Christ's coming through the lens of John's life event. The Bible story in turn provided the basis for John and the group to reflect on their life events and struggles through the lens of faith. They used the Bible story as a mirror and entered into partnership with the story. They saw in the story how God acts in life, and they envisioned and anticipated how they would cooperate with God.

Using scripture passages that are already provided in printed lesson materials is a helpful way of engaging Scripture in the story-linking process. However, if this approach is used, it is important to give specific thought to how the passage applies to a specific area of the everyday life story of African Americans. The leader/teacher will need to review the passage and the lesson material to glean from it the particular factor in African American life it addresses and what specific guidance it might provide. This is looking at Scripture through contextual lenses. This is done *in preparation* for a group session and is done *in tandem* with the selection or creation of case study material. This is important in order that participants may see in the Scripture God's actions in the liberation and vocation of early Christians and what this action has to say for them.

The leader/teacher may also develop the story-linking process focused on a Bible story or text that responds to particular issues raised in the life facet she or he chooses for consideration. As in the preceding situation, the leader/teacher probes the Scripture using contextual lenses. She or he chooses both case studies and Bible texts that illustrate everyday struggles. The Scripture is chosen specifically because it addresses concretely the nature of God's action with which the African American Christian is being called to cooperate in order to bring about liberation and vocation.

Another approach to selecting Scripture is to draw on the biblical frames of reference used by Christian education participants. Participants in Christian education who have a long history of Bible study and reliance on the Bible for life direction may operate quite naturally out of a biblical frame of reference. Often beginning in childhood, these persons have gained knowledge and understandings of the Bible and have looked to the Bible to address the realities of their lives. They are able to cite specific Bible stories or the roles of certain Bible characters that have directed their experiences and behavior.

In order to use this approach, the leader/teacher needs to be aware that there are participants in the group who have developed a biblical frame of reference. If this is known, the leader/teacher may invite persons to share Bible passages that have given them direction in specific situations. The leader/teacher may also select Bible stories that address directly the life situation under discussion. In both instances, however, it is important to have on hand a set of Bible commentaries to assist in the exploration of the biblical material. Some examples of how Bible passages may be used in the story-linking process will appear in upcoming chapters.

Five activities are suggested as means of guiding participants in phase two of the story-linking process. In these activities, the Bible story is disclosed; participants focus on the story or text as mirror; they enter into partnership with the characters of the Bible story;

they envision God's action today; and they anticipate their ongoing response to God.

PHASE THREE: *Engaging Christian Faith Stories from the African American Heritage*

Phase three of the story-linking process is designed to link components of the everyday life story with African American Christian faith heritage stories. The members of John's Sunday school class connected their reflections not only with Scripture but also with their African American foreparents. The group gained additional understanding of and inspiration from the Christian faith story in the Bible by looking at how predecessors in their cultural group responded to it. This activity became an important part of their story-linking process. They recognized that other African Americans before them endeavored to live lives that were formed and informed by this biblical story. They recognized that their predecessors' journeys were difficult but that did not thwart their Christian resolve. They found in the faith-heritage connection an ethical stance on which Christian decisions and actions were made and could still be made even when persons experience their backs against the wall. In short, African American Christian faith heritage stories convey to African Americans today how the Christian life can be lived faithfully. These stories convey to us a liberation mind-set that was at the center of the Christian life of African Americans in the past and that is worthy of emulation in the present. The stories also describe liberation and Christian vocational strategies used in the past that are instructive for the present.

How do we choose the story? There are numerous collections of literature focused on African American history that tell of the religious lives of our predecessors. In choosing what to use in the story-linking process, however, it is important to identify those sources in which the stories are told by African Americans themselves. It is important to be aware that stories may be told in a variety of ways and through a variety of approaches. This means that we should not be hesitant in seeking and using stories, music, sermons, poems, prayers, and artwork that give voice to the African American Christian faith heritage. Some examples will be used in upcoming chapters.

Christian education participants will also have knowledge of heritage stories that they have been taught and that have provided past insight and encouragement to them. These stories will include not only stories of African American heroes and heroines well known to most African Americans but also stories of family heroes and heroines. This personal treasury of heritage stories should not be overlooked. Rather, these stories bring added meaning and depth to the story-linking process.

Three activities are suggested as means of guiding participants in phase three of the story-linking process. The activities are aimed toward assisting participants in identifying how African American predecessors lived out the Christian faith story found in Scripture. In these activities, the Christian faith heritage story is disclosed; participants describe the liberation mind-set found in the story; and they describe the liberation and vocational strategy found in the story.

PHASE FOUR: *Engaging in Christian Ethical Decision Making*

Activities in phase four of the story-linking process are designed to guide persons in exploring options for liberative and Christian vocational actions that have constructive outcomes for them and others. In this phase, persons bring to bear on their life stories ideas, insights, and discernment from the first three phases of the story-linking process.

John and other class members reflected critically on what they were being called to be and to do as Christians. They let the Christian faith story guide them. They acknowledged God's liberating action in John's situation and in their own lives. As African Americans, they wrestled with what it might mean to be faithful Christians amidst uncertainty and struggle. They decided what was responsible and right for them to do as Christians, and they committed themselves to carrying out the actions. In making this commitment, they engaged in Christian ethical decision making activities.

If Christian education activities are to result in liberation and vocation, they must, necessarily, include faithful and responsible Christian action. These activities assume that we as African Americans have a continuing stake in the liberation of others.

We move toward being faithful and responsible as well as toward liberation and vocation as we claim the story of God and the Good News of Jesus Christ found in the Bible as our own. But above all, we move in this direction when we allow ourselves to be shaped by that story and are assured that God is acting in our lives. It means discerning and reflecting critically on how we may intentionally cooperate with this activity. And it means deciding on what and how we will be and act in partnership with God and knowing why. When we engage ourselves in these ways, we are wholly involved in Christian ethical decision making.

Participants become involved in two activities in phase four. In these activities, they discern God's call for concrete liberative and vocational action, and they decide concrete actions.

A Summary of the Entire Story-Linking Process

The story-linking process entails four phases that follow in sequence. Activities facilitate each phase and are designed to be followed in sequence. The entire process need not be covered in one session. If you choose to complete all four phases in one session, it should take about one and one-half hours. If you prefer shorter time segments, complete phases one and two in one session and phases three and four in the next session. The total process is shown below. It is further illustrated in chapters 2, 3, and 4.

PHASE ONE: Engaging the Everyday Story
    Activity 1. Disclose the Everyday Story
    Activity 2. Critically Reflect on the Case Material
    Activity 3. Identify with the Case Study

PHASE TWO: Engaging the Christian Faith Story in the Bible
    Activity 1. Disclose the Bible Story/Text
    Activity 2. Focus on the Bible Story as Mirror
    Activity 3. Enter as Partner with Bible Story Actors
    Activity 4. Envision God's Activity Today
    Activity 5. Anticipate Ongoing Response to God

PHASE THREE: Engaging Christian Faith Stories from the
African American Heritage
Activity 1. Disclose the Faith Heritage Story
Activity 2. Describe the Liberation Mind-set
Activity 3. Describe Liberation and Vocational Strategies

PHASE FOUR: Engaging in Christian Ethical Decision
Making
Activity 1. Discern God's Call for Concrete Action
Activity 2. Decide Concrete Actions

CHAPTER 2 _____

Exploring Self
and World Through
Story-Linking

*Often it is most difficult to accept our fact. Such acceptance means
to say "yes" to that which is our own bill of particulars. . . . It means
being very specific about ourselves. This is our face, not another's; it
will always be our face exhibiting a countenance that reveals all the
laughter and all the tears of our years of living. . . . No substitute can
be found for it—go wherever we will, knock at every door, our face
remains our face.*

—*HOWARD THURMAN*
THE INWARD JOURNEY

Τ he African American story is about a people who continue to ask, Who am I? in the midst of society's assaults to their dignity. The question, Who am I?,
centers on our self-identity, and that identity is shaped
in our homes, communities, and churches, as well as in the larger
social context.

When we arrive at positive notions of our self-identity, we regard
ourselves as valued human beings. As Christians, this means we
see ourselves through the eyes of God found in Jesus Christ revealed in Scripture. We see our lives as gifts from God, and we see

what we have to give to others. Our positive self-identity liberates us to be positive forces in the lives of others. It frees us to be in vocation. Our negative self-identity blocks our ability to be positive forces in others' lives. It blocks our vocation.

Where and how do we develop our self-identities? The answer lies in a critical consciousness of the world we live in because the social contexts of our lives inform how we regard ourselves. We must be attentive to the positive views liberated in us in spite of assaults to our value and dignity and equally aware of self-views that counter the value God places on us, thereby blocking our liberation and vocation. Our challenge is to build on the positives and see our need to be freed from the negatives. Our challenge is to seek an ongoing inner surety of our human value based on knowing deeply God's value of *all* persons revealed in Scripture.

In this chapter, we enter the story-linking process by examining the formation of our identities in our social contexts. We will look at our self-identity stories in light of two case studies—one of an African American female and one of an African American male. Our purpose is to become conscious of whether the self-views we have formed in our social contexts foster or inhibit our own and others' liberation and vocation.

We will link our self-identity stories with a Bible passage with which African Americans resonate because of its focus on identity struggles in difficult and oppressive social contexts. We will also link with a faith heritage story that encapsulates the nature of the African American self-identity struggle and presents a faith response to the struggle.

An important assumption underlies this chapter. The assumption is that when we value ourselves the way God values us, we open ourselves to a variety of dimensions of liberation. We begin to see possibilities we had not heretofore imagined. We become better able to perceive not only who and Whose we are, but also who we can become. We also open ourselves to vocation, which is our response to God's call to care for others.

We learned earlier that the story-linking process has four phases, each of which incorporates several activities. The disclosure of two case studies begins the process in phase one.

PHASE ONE: *Engaging the Everyday Story*

The case study material presented below and case material in subsequent chapters will help us focus on self-identity, social context, interpersonal relationships, life events, and life meanings. However, specific attention is given here to the nature and formation of self-identity in social contexts. The names in the case studies are fictitious.

CASE STUDY 1: *Mary Johnson's Story*

When I talked with Mary Johnson in her home, she watched her daughter at the desk across the room. The desk was filled with opened books and her daughter was busily writing a paper for school. Mary's face shone with pride as she told about her daughter's hard work and academic accomplishments. She shared:

"You know, it's not easy for our young people today. Well, I guess it never has been. But, my husband Bill and I have done our best to provide for our children. We've prayed a lot. It's not easy being parents either. But, when you're a parent—well, you have to *be* a parent. There are things in my life that I wish I could have changed, but being the mother of my children isn't one of them. All in all, I've found being a parent is rewarding. I'd have to say that I'm probably my most caring self as mother.

"I remember when I was growing up. My parents always said, 'Never forget to stand up straight and hold your head up. Be proud of who you are.' It wasn't just a thing of posture. They were letting me know that I was a worthwhile person and that I had a heritage to be proud of. Their words have remained with me and I've tried to instill the same in my children. One thing I also learned from my parents and in church is that other people can try to stop us, but we can't let them. We can't escape the fact that we're African Americans. That's who we are. And, even though living life in these skins of ours is not easy, we know God made us this way and we're valuable in God's sight. I'm a teacher, too, and I try to get this across to my students.

"Oh, I've run into obstacles along the way. And I can't deny

51

that, at times, they made a real mark on my self-image. I remember when students were being considered for the National Honor Society in the predominantly white high school I attended. I was always on the honor roll and participated in a lot of school activities. My goal was to be tops, and I was a high achiever. But I was not chosen for the Honor Society. I found out that some of my white classmates whose grade averages were lower than mine were chosen. It was a terrible blow to me. I can remember crying and crying on my bed at home. I hated who I was, and I frankly thought, 'Why bother ever trying to excel and to be somebody again.' All my parents' talk about standing up straight and being proud went out the window, at least at that specific point in time.

"But, the main thing was that I really didn't let the situation in that high school stop me cold. In fact, I credit that situation with pushing me toward becoming a teacher. I wanted to be in a position to help others and, when I could, to counter negative influences on their lives.

"There were other things, too. How I thought about myself for a long time had a lot to do with an experience at home early in my life. When I was four or five years old, my brother suddenly stopped relating to me. He would not talk to me, sit beside me, or come near me in any way. His treatment of me didn't change until I was grown. I didn't understand why this was happening and whenever I would ask, my parents would simply tell me not to let it bother me. I felt as though there was something terribly wrong with me. And I felt abandoned by my brother, whom I idolized.

"It was not until I was grown that I found out that my brother had been taken aside and severely scolded for playing too roughly with me. His response to the scolding was to completely ignore me for fear of getting into trouble again. But I do think that because of what happened, I'm much more demonstrative in showing affection than I might have been otherwise. And, I think it made me sensitive to others' needs to be included and loved. I also think the whole thing had a big effect on my brother's estimation of himself. Even today, it is hard for him to show affection to anyone. He really became a bottled-up person.

"There are things I have done, too, both good and not so good, that have affected how I think about myself. I mean, some of the things I have chosen to do, like my volunteer work at a senior center some years ago, gave me a kind of peace within myself and positive acceptance of myself as having something to give. At other times, I have not felt okay within myself because I wasn't doing all I could do to help myself and other people, or because I had done something wrong and hadn't set things straight.

"I wrestle with myself even now—with who I am, what I ought to be, and how to get unstuck when I get into one of those places that triggers self-doubt. Deep down inside, though, I see myself as a good person. And, even when I have doubts, I know that God knows who I am. Regardless what others think or do and, really, regardless of my own getting in my own way, I believe God sees me as valuable. I just need to be reminded about that every now and then. And, I need to be reminded that God is there for me when I come upon those obstacles that bring about self-doubt."

CASE STUDY 2: *Ken Brown's Story*

Seated in my office, Ken Brown leaned forward, then back, and heaved many quiet long sighs as he began to tell his story.

"There's no doubt about it, getting this far in my life has been hard; and I'm still young. In my family, I was the youngest of seven children. My dad died when I was about three years old. So basically, my mom had her hands full. We lived on the poor side of town. I mean it was *real poor.* Mom worked in a dry cleaners and my oldest sister worked part-time after she got out of high school each day. She also worked on weekends. Even so, it just wasn't enough. There's not much to say about who we were, except that we were poor and we felt like we were society's castaways. We were trying to make it against all odds.

"We wore hand-me-down clothes that were beyond mending, and we didn't always have shoes that kept our feet off the ground, if you know what I mean. We had food stamps, but, still, food stretching was an ordinary thing; and my mother always talked about how nasty the store clerks were when she would hand them the stamps.

"I can remember Mom was a proud person and she tried to do her best with us kids. She tried to make us behave. She tried to make us stay in school. She tried to make us study. Sometimes, she'd get very upset with us kids—you know how kids can be and what it must have been like to have seven of us. But she'd always say, 'Everything's gonna be all right. We're gonna make it with God's help.' If there ever was a person who had hope, she was it. I can't say that I believed as she did when I was growing up. It just seemed to me then that we got the raw end of the deal in life. We didn't go to church or Sunday school or anything like that, but we always said grace at the dinner table. I also remember many times hearing Mom praying while she was fixing a meal, trying to clean up the house, and doing other things around the house. Now that I think of it, I guess she had to pray in order for her to keep going in a house with seven kids.

"I really believe my Mom's pride, her hope, her desire for the best for all of us, and her prayers made a difference in my life. It didn't seem to make a difference for some of my brothers and sisters, but it did for me. Now, I did get into my share of mischief, especially in elementary school, and I was suspended several times. But I know something must have made a difference because I made it through school. Or maybe I should say I chose to survive in a different way. I'm the only one in my family who became a church-goer. Don't get me wrong, I don't fault them. It's just that there's something I've got to do. I've committed my life as a Christian to ministry with young people in situations like mine.

"I know some folk don't think anything good can come out of the poor section of town, and that poor folk don't help themselves or anybody else. That may be true for some. But that's not true for all. There are proud, hardworking, poor folk who want things to be different and who are working to make things different for themselves and others. My Mom was one of those folk. And so am I. I am worried about several of my brothers and sisters, though, because they can't seem to get beyond all the negatives. It is sometimes hard not to get discouraged when I think of them. I do what I can, but sometimes I think, 'How can I feel good about being who I am now when they are having such trouble?' "

ACTIVITY 1—*Disclose the Everyday Story*

Use of prerecorded tapes of the case studies using African American voices is a helpful method of presentation. Participants may also read the cases aloud—a female for Mary's story and a male for Ken's story. Or, leader(s)/teacher(s) may read them.

Prior to presenting the cases, invite participants to listen for evidence of positive and negative self-perceptions of Mary and Ken. Encourage participants to:

* listen for the social contexts—the home, community, church, workplace, school—in which Mary's and Ken's self-perceptions arose;
* locate circumstances under which the self-perceptions arose;
* give particular attention to where and in what ways Mary's and Ken's self-identity blocked their enactment of vocation and where and what changes in their self-identity liberated this enactment.

Participants should be free to identify issues regarding self-identity the cases raise for them.

ACTIVITY 2—*Critically Reflect on the Case Material*

In activity 2 of phase one of the story-linking process, participants respond to the listening cues indicated above. The approach used for sharing depends on the size of the group and their readiness for open group sharing. In large groups, it is helpful to talk in small groups followed by small group report-backs. In situations where there is a fair amount of reticence in open group sharing, persons may share with a partner. Each small group or pair may choose a reporter to convey insights to the larger group.

Reflection Exercise. Consider your responses to the case studies based on the listening cues given above. Some actual participant responses are as follows:

Self-Identity in Social Context and Liberation and
Vocation of Mary Johnson

Mary's present self-identity is tied to her role as mother in the context of home and to the role of teacher in the context of the school. There is a sense in which she is bound to these roles and either cannot envision or did not choose to mention an identity in other contexts.

The foundation for Mary's self-identity was laid in the home where she grew up. That foundation had to do with the way she was to present herself, posturally—holding the head high and standing up straight. But it also had to do with maintaining pride in her heritage, who she is as an African American, and seeing herself as valued because God made her the way she is. However, this foundation was challenged in the home and school contexts. Finding a block to her self-identity in school was not surprising. Finding a block in the home was an important reminder that our identities are not formed in just one place.

For a long time, Mary needed liberation from her negative views acquired in the home and school. Her story shows that she somehow got a vision of herself as a caring person and as teacher. She actualized this vision in her home and school. In this way, her vision may be described as a liberating vision and her enactment of it may be described as her liberation to vocation. We can guess that her early foundation may have made a difference. But we cannot tell whether she came out of a strong positive self-perception or from one that isn't as strong as it might be. It raises the issue of how strong a person's self-identity has to be in order for them to move toward and fulfill vocation credibly. But, even when persons have a less then strong self-identity, it does not have to be crippling. Isn't it possible that a person can accomplish a lot in spite of a weak self-identity or even because of it?

Self-Identity in Social Context and Liberation and
Vocation of Ken Brown

Ken identified himself as a Christian survivor. In this way, he came to a positive view of himself in spite of the views he felt others held of him and his family. Ken definitely internalized the negative views toward the poor found in the larger social context. He may have even taken on these views and "worn them like a badge." This perhaps figured into his acting out and being suspended from school. But, like Mary, he was able to build on a foundation that he received in the home that included the views that persons are important to God.

Ken experienced liberation to vocation in spite of his bombardment with negative views from the larger social context. He envisioned a call to take on the identity of minister in order to confront the concerns for a positive self-identity faced by other African Americans. The foundation that was built in the home where Ken grew up contributed to his liberation. But, unlike Mary, he mentioned that one dimension of liberation for him came through religious transformation. This seems to have been highly instrumental in his overcoming the blocks of negative self-identity because with it he received a new identity.

There is a question, though, about whether Ken will be overwhelmed with his new identity and whether he will feel guilty for having it to the degree that it becomes as restrictive as a negative self-perception. His story raises the issue of whether our liberation from an old negative identity to a new positive one can be threatening and even scary.

ACTIVITY 3—*Identify with the Case Study*

In activity 3, I invite participants to disclose what the cases evoked in them about their own self-perceptions. Starter questions for this disclosure include:

* In what ways are Mary's and Ken's story your story?
* What memories of self-perceptions and social contexts did their stories trigger in you?
* How would you respond to the issues that were raised?

Follow-up questions might include: Did anyone have difficulty relating to the stories? What was difficult? Why was it difficult?

I have found that people tend to key into one specific aspect of one of the case studies. Some identify with the positive self-perception found in Mary's or Ken's case study and then build on that perception to describe how they consider themselves and who contributed to it. Others identify with a particular place, such as Mary's high school, as a way of talking about the social context in which they themselves confronted blocks and formed negative self-perceptions. Participants also tend to use Mary's becoming a teacher and Ken's moving toward ministry with youths as ways of talking about what they themselves are or are not doing with regard to vocation. Some persons also disclose difficulties they themselves have or that others have in arriving at a positive self-identity in social context. And persons speak of the importance of the church's role as well as its problems in building positive self-identity. Groups will, of course, differ in their responses.

Reflection Exercise. What did the cases evoke in you?

PHASE TWO: *Engaging the Christian Faith Story in the Bible*

The intent in phase two of the story-linking process is to link Mary's, Ken's, and our own reflections of the cases with Scripture. We seek guidance from Scripture on the formation of self-identity in social context from a Christian standpoint. Our search is accomplished through five activities including linking with a specific Scripture, focusing on the Scripture as mirror, entering into partnership with Bible-story actors, envisioning God's action today, and anticipating ongoing response to God. Psalm 139 is used here to illustrate a manner of linking with Scripture.

Psalm 139 is a particularly helpful Bible passage for African Americans' exploration of self-identity. In the face of ongoing bombardment of African Americans with negative views from the larger social context and assaults to self-identity elsewhere, the psalm proposes a counter-view. It grants African Americans an identity that is not tied to what humans ascribe to it. It anchors identity in God.

ACTIVITY 1—*Disclose the Bible Story/Text*

I invite persons to enter Psalm 139 by considering the questions: Why Psalm 139? What does Psalm 139 have to contribute to our understanding of our self-identities as African Americans in the social contexts described in the case studies and in our own lives? These questions provide specific listening cues.

The self-identities of Mary and Ken were formed in contexts where there were both positive experiences and anguished experiences of hurt, alienation, and suffering. Along the way, they both arrived at positive notions of the self, but there were also instances in which those notions were challenged. However, both Mary and Ken saw God as Guarantor of their positive self-identity. But they needed to know that this Guarantor can be counted on in the face of doubt and experiences that challenge positive self-identity. The experiences of Mary and Ken are not unlike our own.

I also add that the formation of self-identity in the social contexts in the case studies and the formation of our own self-identity in our social contexts are not unique to us. The important question of, Who am I? and where and how that question gets answered have been posed throughout the history of humankind. It was posed during biblical times. The psalmist who wrote Psalm 139 was among the ancient Israelites who had experienced the troubling and disorienting wilderness sojourn of a people in the years following their exodus from Egypt. The trials and tribulations pushed the psalmist to consider the question of identity. Psalm 139 reveals the psalmist's conversation with God about the answer to the question, Who am I in the context in which I find myself?

Participants then hear Psalm 139. There are many creative ways to present Scripture. It may be presented on prerecorded audiotape using a single African American voice or several African American voices. It may be read responsively from the Bible, with the leader/teacher and the participants reading alternate verses, or it may be read collectively from large printed placards or newsprint centrally located in a meeting room. Take some time now to read Psalm 139.

ACTIVITY 2—*Focus on the Bible as Mirror*

Invite persons into a second reading of the psalm. During this reading, persons approach the psalm as a mirror in their further exploration of answers to the questions: Who are Mary, Ken, and I in our social contexts? Who is our church and our community? We also consider how the psalm can assist us in our liberation struggle and our exercise of vocation. Guide this kind of exploration by inviting persons to find in the psalm motifs or words that suggest answers. Invite them to describe how these motifs challenge our understanding of liberation and vocation and to voice their own questions that the psalm raises.

Reflection Exercise. Take some time now to re-read Psalm 139 to discover your responses.

Responses summarized from actual participants and commentaries are as follows:

"The psalm is saying that Mary, Ken, and we have an identity that does not come from what other people say or do in our social contexts. That identity is found in God. The God that the psalmist speaks about is *One who has depthful knowledge about who we are and what happens to us.*" (verses 1-12)

"Regardless of our social contexts, God is always with us, before us, over us, and surrounding us. God leads and holds God's people of faith even in the most difficult trials and tribulations of life. We are transparent to God and known by God, because *God created us.*" (verses 13-16)

"Because we recognize that God created us and knows us, there is nowhere we can go and nothing that can happen to us that can separate our being from God's being. *In God is our identity and our life.*" (verses 17-18)

"God provides a protective reality or a 'sacred canopy' under which we can feel completely known, secure, affirmed, and loved even in the midst of social contexts that are threatening. Under this 'sacred canopy' *God hears our prayers and innermost cries.*" (verses 19-24)[1]

"God knows us better than we know ourselves. God knows us in a different way than those around us know us. And God knows us longer and deeper than any other. Our identities *are* more, *can be* more, than those which are already known about us.[2] When we see our identity through God's eyes, we are freed to *be* more and to act out of that being. We no longer see our social contexts as binding us."

"The psalm challenges us to look more closely at our self-perceptions and our social contexts. We are challenged to address what is preventing us from grounding our identity in God. Of what help is it if we ground our identities in God's and feel liberated by that grounding, but do not seek to change anything in the world? This is a question of our vocation.

ACTIVITY 3—*Enter as Partner with Bible-Story Actors*

We begin the third activity by imaging ourselves standing or sitting with the psalmist. From this stance, we enter into conversation with God along with the psalmist as though the words of Psalm 139 are our own. We then recite the psalm from this partnership stance.

A particularly helpful way of entering this partnership with the psalmist is for two persons to read the psalm together. In pairs, one would assume the role of the psalmist, while the other reads from his/her own personal stance. After the reading, the partners would exchange roles.

Reflection Exercise. Imagine yourself as a partner with the psalmist. Read the words of the psalm as though they were your words being said in partnership with the psalmist.

ACTIVITY 4—*Envision God's Activity Today*

Invite persons to envision God's action in forming and informing our self-identities in our social contexts. This envisioning process may be accomplished through one or more of the following: (1) Persons may enter into a time of silent reflection in which they envision God's affirming their identity in God. (2) Persons may be invited to share their responses to the impact of reading Psalm 139 as though it were their own words and in partnership with the psalmist. (3) Persons may be asked to write and share a prayer, a poem, choose a song to sing, draw a picture, or construct a group collage from magazine pictures or original pictures.

These activities should convey something of the meanings persons assign to identities that are grounded in God and their feelings about those meanings. For example, in one instance, the psalm confirmed for a person the meaning of a favorite African American gospel song entitled "God Is." The person then shared the words: "God is the joy and the strength of my life."

Reflection Exercise. Choose and complete one of the three exercises above.

ACTIVITY 5—*Anticipate Ongoing Response to God*

In this final activity of phase two, I invite persons to anticipate their response to God's call to individuals and churches to anchor self-identity in God. This entails identifying negative self-perceptions God is calling us to release, both individually and as church. Some starter questions that are helpful to ask are: What negative perceptions do you have of yourself that hinder your acting in liberating ways or in vocation in your various social contexts? How did God speak to you through the case studies to challenge you to release negative self-perceptions? How did God speak to you through the psalm to challenge you to release negative self perceptions? How is your church challenged by the psalm?

Forming the participants in pairs or in small groups can facilitate sharing in this activity of the story-linking process. Or persons may engage in this activity meditatively. Some persons find it helpful to record what they discern in a journal. If there are persons who wish to share what they discern, however, they should not be prevented from doing so.

Reflection Exercise. Take some time to meditate on what God is saying to you about your self-identity.

Some actual participant responses are as follows:

"I've always had to work on my perception of myself as not having the ability to measure up. This stems, in part, from an experience in school. When I failed to read a sentence correctly, I was told to sit down and that I 'didn't know beans from potatoes.' For a long time, it blocked my ability to read. I have also had trouble believing in myself, and I tend not to put a great deal of effort into things for fear of failure."

"I am challenged to stop crying over the negative way others define me. I've cried long enough. Sometimes it's hard, but I do have the power to look beyond the words that tear me down. I don't have to let others' opinions become my reality. I also have the responsibility to counter negative comments I hear being made about us whenever I hear them. I also know that I'm not perfect and God knows that too. I have both the power and the responsibility to shape up what isn't right."

"It is important that my church be an affirming place. It's a small struggling church, and we get down on ourselves a lot. Unless we see ourselves in the right light, we can't carry out any adequate kind of vocation. I believe that and think church members are called to a better way of seeing ourselves so we can do ministry in a better way."

PHASE THREE: *Engaging Christian Faith Stories from the African American Heritage*

In phase three of the story-linking process, we link with an African American Christian faith heritage story. Many stories are possible for this stage. What I call Grandmother's Message About Identity as told by Howard Thurman will be used here to illustrate how this linkage can occur in an actual Christian education setting. The story is particularly conducive to the African American focus on self-identity in a story-linking process because it shows vividly the similarity between the self-identity struggle of our foreparents and our own struggle. But, more than this, it conveys forcefully our value in God's eyes by daring to utter the opposite view we hear regularly. Grandmother's Message About Identity may be told in this way:

> When I was a youngster, this [sense of identity through God's love] was drilled into me by my grandmother. The idea was given to her by a certain slave minister who, on occasion, held secret religious meetings with his fellow slaves. How everything in me quivered with the pulsing tremor of raw energy when, in her recital, she would come to the triumphant climax of the minister: "You—you are not niggers. You—you are not slaves. You are God's children."

63

SOUL STORIES

This brief story becomes the basis for the following two activities of phase three: linking with the African American heritage story and describing the liberation mind-set and liberation and vocational strategy.

ACTIVITY 1—*Disclose the Faith Heritage Story*

I simply invite persons to enter the context in which Howard Thurman recalls his Grandmother's Message About Identity. We imagine ourselves to be in the grandparent's home. I assign half of the participants to take Howard Thurman's role as narrator and to read the words that introduced what his grandmother said. The other half is asked to read incisively and dramatically grandmother's precise repetition of the minister's words. Very often, I will ask the two groups to reverse roles, so that each group has a chance to be both the narrator and the grandmother.

ACTIVITY 2—*Describe the Liberation Mind-set and Liberation and Vocational Strategy*

Here we explore the liberation mind-set and the liberation and vocational strategy in Grandmother's Message About Identity. This is done first by considering how Psalm 139 is reflected in the story, given the social context in which it is cast. Persons often respond to this invitation by saying that the story lets us know as African Americans that, in spite of the social context in which we feel enslaved, devalued or denigrated, we are God's creations.

To invite further reflection, additional questions are posed: How may Grandmother's Message About Identity create a liberation mind-set in persons? How may the message help us to see ourselves positively and act on that positive view? Is there more that is needed than the story provides to help create in us a liberating mind-set? If so, what is needed?

Reflection Exercise. Take some time now to think about your answers to the above questions.
Actual response of one participant:

"The dominant mind-set was one of staunch maintenance of a counterview of self than the one often given to us. The message is a helpful one in that there is a sense in which it is being passed on and on from one generation to another. It reminds me of Jesse Jackson's words, 'I am somebody!' It suggests a strategy of reciting over and over again the countermessage, 'We are God's children!' and, 'I am somebody!' At the same time, there is more to it than simply saying the words. We have to believe it deep down inside. And to come to believe it, we have to keep struggling to combat all the negatives that knock us down and that have an impact on our negative views of ourselves. That is key!"

PHASE FOUR: *Engaging in Christian Ethical Decision Making*

The aim in the last phase of the story-linking process is decision making regarding actions that can liberate ongoing positive self-identity. To do this, we propose possible and plausible actions that emerge from our discernment of God's call for action.

ACTIVITY 1—*Discern God's Call*

We begin by engaging in what I refer to as "silent memory summation." This entails our calling to memory, silently, as much as we can about Psalm 139 and the story of Grandmother's Message About Identity. After our silent memory summation, I invite group members to choose a partner. The partners share specific points in the psalm and in Grandmother's Message About Identity that motivate them and their church to address negative self-identities among African Americans. Partners also share specific social contexts in which they and their churches are called to act.

Reflection Exercise. Enter into the silent memory summation. What in Psalm 139 and Grandmother's Message About Identity motivates you to action and where are you being called to act?

Actual responses of participants are as follows:

"I was motivated by the psalmist's confirmation that wherever I go, God is with me. That is a double-edged motivation for me. I know that if I sit down and do nothing to make possible our

65

young people's positive self-identity, I will be seen and judged by God. At the same time, doing something is a hard thing. Yet, I know that there is a God who wants us to know ourselves as valued even if there are humans who don't want us to and are working to assure that we don't know ourselves. There's a lot that needs to be done in our schools to promote positive valuing of our heritage and our children's positive sense of self. I feel God is calling me to address this in the school where my children go. This is also an area where the church can get involved."

"The word *nigger* still stings deep in my soul. For Howard Thurman's grandmother to speak it aloud in order to affirm what we are not was tremendously motivating. She had to have known deep in her soul the meaning of Psalm 139. Anyway, I often hear that derogatory term from the lips of our young people, as though it were an affectionate term. That bothers me. I think one of the places both the Scripture and Grandmother's story is calling me to act is right where we live—in our homes, in our communities, and in our churches, to confront the use of the term there."

ACTIVITY 2—*Decide Concrete Actions*

In the final activity of the story-linking process, two sets of partners combine into a small group of four. In small groups, we decide specific responses to God's call to address negative self-identities and social contexts in which the responses will be made. We begin by answering the following questions: If you could fashion the most positive self-identity for African Americans of any age, what would it look like? What qualities would form a positive self-identity?

When this question is answered, we brainstorm every context in which action is needed to liberate within persons in an ongoing way the positive self-identity we have described. The groups then choose one specific social context in which to design a programmatic response. Finally, the groups identify a specific kind of program and steps that their church can realistically undertake to accomplish the positive self-identity they have described. Groups also choose songs and scriptures that inspire action. A song example is the spiritual, "This Little Light of Mine."[4] A Scripture example is Matthew 5:14-16. The small group proposals are then shared with the total group.

Providing additional hints for addressing self-negating social contexts is a helpful follow-up to group proposals. Examples of such hints are as follows:

"Find another caring person to tell about experiences that threaten your positive self-identity. This can be someone in the church, home, community, school, or workplace. Moreover, be a caring other to someone else and help to form a caring network in the church community."

"Cultivate a viable faith perspective. This means being aware of what we believe and have experienced about God through Jesus Christ in our lives. It also means taking note of our devotional practices—prayer and meditation, Bible study, and worship— wherein we are opened to God's presence and affirming activity in our lives."

"Identify with an exemplar of the Christian faith. Seek inspiration from and become a partner with a person in the Bible or in the Christian faith heritage who exemplifies what it means to form and act on positive self-identity."

"Keep alert to feelings of self-negation and image pathways to addressing positive self-identity in distressing social contexts."

"Become partners with others in envisioning ways of confronting self-negating social contexts and in acting to bring about affirming social contexts."

Follow-up Suggestions

In a follow-up session, invite participants to share case illustrations, using fictitious names, of African Americans they know who are struggling to maintain positive self-identities in self-negating social contexts. Possible alternative scriptures for follow-up sessions include Genesis 16:1-6, 21:8-21; II Corinthians 5:17; Matthew 5:13-20; and Romans 8:12-18. These are Scriptures that address self-identity struggles in difficult and oppressive contexts. An alternate approach to the African American Christian faith heritage story is to invite participants to share stories told by older members of their families that confront negative self-identity and seek to build positive self-identity.

The leader/teacher may also invite participants to share cultural sayings that focus on concerns for self and world. One such cultural saying is a commentary on the story of Hagar and Ishmael and refers to Hagar as "Aunt Haggie." The saying is presented in the discussion on Scripture in chapter 5.

Exploring Events of Our Lives Through Story-Linking

When there is that which I would claim as my very own, a second look, a subtle strangeness, something, announces that there can never be anything that is my very own. Always moving in upon life is the friend whose existence [we] did not know, whose coming and going is not [our's] to determine. . . . [Our] life is [our] very own and [our] life is never [ours] alone.

—*HOWARD THURMAN*
THE INWARD JOURNEY

Like self-identity in social contexts, interpersonal relationships and life events are important related dimensions of the everyday stories of African Americans. Therefore, the story-linking process must rightly focus on them. In this chapter, we will consider what interpersonal relationships and life events mean, what they have to do with liberation and vocation, and how they may be addressed in the story-linking process.

Interpersonal Relationships

Interpersonal relationships are the associations and connections we make with other people. We relate to family members, extended family, and friends. We have church, school, and work relationships. We relate in various ways to persons in other social and political institutions of the nation. Moreover, as Christians, we see ourselves in relationship with God through Jesus Christ. In all of these relationships, we hold various roles, behave in various ways, and have particular attitudes and feelings about how and with whom we relate.

We experience some relationships as liberating and some as stifling or paralyzing. We seek liberation from stifling or paralyzing relationships to significant, positive, and wholeness-producing ones. As Christians, our vocational role is that of Christ's helper in bringing about this liberation for us and others. Attitudinally, we view those with whom we relate as creations of God, and we regard them as sisters and brothers.

But we may say, "This is so hard to do! Oppression seems to forever stalk and maim us! And even close relationships wound us!" Our purpose in this chapter is to consider our stories of relationships and to determine ways of fostering liberating and vocation-centered relationships in the midst of relational difficulties. We will do this by reflecting critically on the hard realities of relationships through use of additional case study material from Mary Johnson and Ken Brown. We will link with Scripture for its direction in liberating and vocation-centered relationships. We will also seek direction from an African American Christian faith heritage story.

Life Events

Life events include crises such as illness, hospitalization, disabling conditions, death, unfair treatment, broken relationships, job loss, homelessness, and incarceration. They entail positive incidents such as gratifying memories, life-changing religious experiences, promotions, honors, mended relationships, and reunions. They also include incidents that mark stages of our lives, such as marriage, childbirth, school graduations, separation, divorce, becoming orphaned or widowed, and entering or exiting a chosen life-style or occupation.

Positive life events exhilarate us and free within us a sense of joy. Negative life events trouble us and sometimes bring us to the brink of spiritual and mental paralysis. Joyful events are worthy of celebration in community, and troubling events are needful of caring response by community members. When we celebrate together and care for one another, we are in vocation. For African Americans, this kind of vocation-centeredness builds on the historical cultural view that is traceable to our African ancestry. The view is found in the African proverb, "I am because we are, and since we are, therefore I am." A similar African proverb is, "One is only human because of others, with others, for others."

These proverbs highlight a "we" orientation to life and suggest that liberation and vocation evolve from communal awareness and demonstration of celebratory and caring kinship. In the early history of African Americans, the African ancestral "we" became connected with the Christian faith. It was informed by Divine love attested to in Scripture and generated by an understanding of relationships based on communal love and caring. In the midst of oppressing events and suffering, persons experienced the transformed "we" as liberating. Celebration was possible in the "we" relationships. The "we" relationships freed people from hopelessness and the temptation to give up in the face of profoundly burdensome and painful life events. They were freed to develop a common vision of deliverance from oppressive forces, how to actualize that vision, and how to give support in the process. They were free to be in vocation.

As we enter the story-linking process in this chapter, we will keep alert to life events that call for celebration and ones that call for caring response in the case studies and in our stories. Note the presence or absence of the African American "we" orientation. We will give attention to what Scripture and an African American Christian faith heritage story tell us about liberating and vocation-centered responses to life events.

PHASE ONE: *Engaging the Everyday Story*

The following stories told by Mary Johnson and Ken Brown form the centerpiece for our entering the story-linking process in this chapter. Focus here is on what the new case study material conveys about interpersonal relationships and life events.

CASE STUDY 1: *Mary Johnson's Story*

Pointing to her graying hair, Mary continued her story:

"I guess you'd say I've come of age. No, I'm not what you'd call old, but I'm not what you'd call young either. I'd say I'm dead center in midlife at age forty-seven, and that means I've done a lot of living and that there have been a lot of changes in my life. For instance one of the biggest changes is the loss of my mother. I miss my mother and need her now. I have so many questions I'd like to ask her. In a lot of ways, I would like to be like her, even though there are things she didn't do that I do. She was very much the homemaker, whereas I had the opportunity to become a teacher. But she was always a quiet person but a strong person. I think, though, that she kept a lot inside. She didn't let us in on a lot of things, especially things that were bothering her. In that respect, she was sometimes in her own little world. I wish we could have shared more than we did. I really miss her.

"One thing has happened since my mother's death. I take greater pains to keep in contact with my father. My father is still living and that's a blessing to me. But I know the day will come when he'll be gone, too. Right now, it's important for me, and I think for him, that we stay in touch as much as we can, even though it's not always easy to visit since we live across the country from him. I usually take the tape recorder when I visit because he knows the family history and wants to tell it, and I want to hear it.

"Speaking of people's own little worlds again, I recall a time when our daughter was diagnosed with cancer. She was an infant then. I knew that she was getting good medical care, and she was in a comfortable hospital room. But from a medical standpoint, I also knew she could die. I was so worried. It was like I became walled off in a space of disbelief and worry and grief. Thinking back, I know I felt our daughter was going to come through and that I had faith in God that she would. Really, I did have faith. Yet, I also felt so alone. In that situation, it was our family, our close friends, and the people in our church who made all the difference. They got through to me in my little world. They helped get me through this rough time. I'm so grateful our daughter lives, and I'm grateful for supportive friends. They made me realize how important friends are. They motivated me to be a better friend to those I know.

"Well, as I'm thinking about it, this whole thing about people being in their own little worlds really has many meanings. I think we all have times in our lives when we feel like we're just out there alone. You know, as an African American, my husband Bill did pretty well climbing the corporate ladder. But there still was only so far he could go in the company. He was retired early. The reality is that there are many long-timers in the company like him who have never made it as far as he did. It is like only one or two African Americans are going to make it up the ladder, even though my husband says they're extremely capable and have put in their time. They're kept at lower level jobs.

"The punch line is that they're required to train non-blacks for the next level up. And the non-blacks go up. Now, this is a situation where these black men didn't choose to be in their own little world with no exit. My husband kept putting in a good word for these guys and pulling for them, and there was a comraderie among them. They gave encouragement to one another. But the situation never changed much.

"I really feel like the most important thing in the world is relationships. That's basically what I think. But, it seems some relationships happen that make you feel good. What do you do when they fail?"

CASE STUDY 2: *Ken Brown's Story*

Ken confessed that there was a time when he would have had great difficulty telling his story. But now, he says:

"It's important that I tell it. I've come a long way in my twenty-five years. It reminds me of the road and new problems that are still ahead of me. I know there's no life without problems for me and others. I intend to help other people with theirs.

"Speaking of problems, I can still remember the morning my mom died. I was twelve years old. Mom had battled cancer for a long time. She never was her old self after coming home from the hospital a few weeks before. Anyway, on that morning, I woke up to the sound of anguished cries, shouting, and moans. I knew what had happened. One of my sisters called 911. Two white paramedics came. They became frustrated by all of our crying, which got worse as they covered Mom and started to take her out. They gave us no comfort. Maybe they weren't supposed to. They said to us very sharply and coldly, 'Shut up! Your crying won't do you any good!' Over the years, I've been able to over-come their treatment and insensitivity toward us. But it definitely was hard to take then.

"After Mom's death, I moved around a lot. I lived with foster parents. I lived for short periods with sisters and brothers in different cities. While I was with one of my brothers, I actually saw him shooting drugs. In fact, every one of my sisters and brothers had a problem with drugs or alcohol. One sister is struggling with that problem now and is a single parent with several children. One brother has since been incarcerated.

"I was put out of the home of one of my sisters during a difficult period when she and her husband were on drugs, and he was taking her money. I was fourteen then, and I lived on the streets. I didn't know anything to do but pray. I remembered that Mom always prayed, and she prayed for me before she died. I told God one day when I was lying on a bench in the rain that I knew the worse it could get was that I die, so let me die or make it better. God and I had a good relationship; he helped me when things weren't going right. And God didn't foreclose on me. Time after time, God sent somebody. Someone intervened in my life at my most alienated moment.

"One time when I lived with my brother in another city, I enrolled in a middle school. Instead of being put in the eighth grade where I belonged, I was put in the sixth grade. I went to a magnet school while my mom was living and had managed to accomplish some things very well. So what happened just wasn't fair. Plus I was big for my age. I was embarrassed. I was ready to give up and drop out. I went to a white female counselor who asked me how I got behind. After hearing me read and watching me complete successfully the math problems she gave me, she took me to the black principal's office. He handed me a magazine, and I read it fluently. The counselor showed him my math work. I was then put in the seventh grade, and shortly after into the eighth grade class. But I didn't stay in that school long. I moved in with my sister in another city.

"I enrolled in another school after moving. I had a report card from my previous school. With some testing, I went into the eighth grade. My teacher was very supportive. I worked hard. That teacher bought me a suit for my eighth grade graduation. I moved to a children's home after graduation. I felt secure there. The executive director said that, if I finished high school, she would help me get into college. The school got me tutors and even gave me guitar lessons. Well, I graduated, and the director saw that I entered college. I stopped college studies for a while, but went back after I got married. My wife became my greatest source of inspiration. She still is as I make my way through seminary.

"I know that God had a hand in my life. I often wonder what my life would be like if there hadn't been what I call miracles along the way. The help I've gotten from others has confirmed in my mind that there is a God who works through people to make us whole. I didn't always think this way. As a young kid, I really didn't believe God existed. I also had a lot of anger. Many times I bitterly thought, 'Why is life so hard? Why did Mom have to die?' She was a very good person. I wanted to know, 'Why were we treated so badly?' It occurs to me that maybe my brothers and sisters are struggling with these questions. Perhaps they haven't yet found a way to deal with what happened to Mom and to us when we were young.

"My constant prayer is that my brothers and sisters will somehow find a better way. I try to stay in contact with them. My oldest sister gave her life to Christ. I was recently with her when she had a serious operation. She is doing just fine. But there is a block between me and the others. They push me away because I'm a Christian and tell me they don't want to hear anything I have to say. It's very painful. They're my family, and they mean a lot to me. My greatest prayer is that they won't leave here before things are right between them and God and between them and me."

ACTIVITY 1—*Disclose the Everyday Story*

The new case material may be presented through prerecorded audiotapes using African American voices. It may also be read aloud by participants—a female for Mary Johnson's story and a male for Ken Brown's story, or, the leader(s)/teacher(s) may read it.

In an actual Christian education setting, I invite persons in advance of the case disclosures to consider what is conveyed about: interpersonal relationships; liberating and vocation-centered versus paralyzing roles, behaviors, and attitudes; life events calling for celebration and ones calling for caring response, and evidences of a "we" orientation.

ACTIVITY 2—*Critically Reflect on the Case Material*

Present the following questions to invite participants to share their responses to the case material:

* What relationships are stifling or paralyzing? How?
* What relationships are positive and produce wholeness?
* What events call for caring responses? Why?
* What events call for celebration? Why?
* Where do you see evidence of liberation and vocation or blocks to them?

As indicated earlier, the strategy used for sharing depends on the group size and openness to sharing. In large groups, subgroups of three to four persons may be formed. They may report back upon conclusion of the sharing period. In situations where there is reticence of persons to share, I invite persons to choose a partner. After a period of partner sharing, two sets of partners may combine. A recorder from the group of four may then report the group's insights to the larger group.

Reflection Exercise. Reflect on the case studies and respond to the questions provided above.

The following are responses given by actual participants.

Responses to Mary's Story

"Mary thinks relationships are the most important thing in the world. Her story proves it. She had a positive relationship with her mother. She still seems to be grieving her death. This loss as well as her daughter's illness brought about real crisis events that called for caring response. She's right that friendship is essential. She needed it. We all do, especially in times of crisis. Sometimes it takes a real friend to break through the kind of isolation Mary talked about during her time of crisis. In her case, it was the only way to move from her 'I' to the 'We' her friends saw that she needed."

"Mary's mother chose isolation at points in her life when she was apparently dealing with tough events. However, in Bill's situation and that of the workers, isolation due to disenfranchisement was thrust upon them. They didn't have a choice. Either way, it can block your liberation."

"It took real vision for Mary to seek out her father to be storyteller. Mary's vocation and her father's, too, came through in her story-listening and her father's storytelling. It must have been freeing for him to know that she cared for him and wanted to hear what he knew about the family history. They developed a good sense of 'we.' This is reason for celebration."

Responses to Ken's Story

"Ken experienced some *big crises*. And, he bumped up against *big blocks* in relationships—the paramedics, school officials, and siblings. It would be easy for those two *bigs* to cause anyone to close everybody out, including God. But persons respond differently to crises and bad relationships. Ken always seemed ready to grab hold of liberating and caring relationships—memory of his mother's relationship with him, good-willed school personnel, his wife. He did not let the blocking ones get him so far down that he couldn't get up. On the other hand, his brothers and sisters took a different approach. They created new crises for themselves through drugs and alcohol. For whatever reasons, they blocked their own liberation, vocation, and ability to enter into significant and meaningful 'we' relationships."

"The paramedics have no excuse for their bad attitudes. How they acted was stifling to the grief-stricken children. But just maybe they were freaked out because of seeing too much death. In any event, the children needed caring from someone. Then, too, they may not have been culturally sensitive."

"Because of the new and liberating relationships forged between key people and Ken, he was freed to get his education, to see the needs of others, and to respond to the vision God gave him for ministry. The church was not part of Ken's early relational network. But he does not say why. Is it possible that churches were blinded to what liberation and vocation meant for those in Ken's neighborhood?"

ACTIVITY 3—*Identify with the Case Study*

After critical reflection on the case studies, I invite participants to share what the case material evoked in them about their own interpersonal relationships and life events. Starter questions include: In what ways did you see yourself in the case material? With what persons, roles, behaviors, and attitudes did you most identify? Why? What responses would you have found liberating given similar life events? How would your church as a corporate body respond to the life events Mary and Ken experienced?

Reflection Exercise. What answers would you give to the preceding questions?

I have found that participants vary in their identification with the case material. Some persons identify with Mary's grief from her mother's death or her caretaking role with her elderly father, while others identify with the father's storytelling role. Others strongly identify with the crisis of the daughter's illness and Mary's distraught response. Still others identify with Mary's support network, with her husband, Bill, or with the workers' relationships and workplace dilemma.

In Ken's story, some persons identify with the events in Ken's early life and with differences in the impact of maiming behaviors and attitudes on Ken versus his siblings. Others identify with the whole of Ken's story and say that it could have been their story. Some persons also see themselves or their family members in Ken's and his siblings' way of relating. Others identify with caring school authorities and overlook the noncaring ones. And persons sometimes recall the church's role or its lack of a role in their lives when they confronted situations similar to Ken's.

Participants typically identify with the stories on the basis of their relationships and critical events in their own lives. They also sometimes recall how their church assisted or did not assist them in crisis situations.

PHASE TWO: *Engaging the Christian Faith Story in the Bible*

Phase two of the story-linking process is concerned with linking case material and participant reflections with Scripture. What guidance does Scripture give about interpersonal relations and life events? By way of illustration, Mark 2:1-12, the story of the paralytic, will be used. This story holds particular significance in terms of interpersonal relationships and life events of African Americans.

The story mirrors the meaning of liberating and vocation-centered relationships. It reveals a "we" response to those who, like African Americans, experienced oppressive events and isolation. This story allows us to identify with the role of the paralytic and to imagine our living out his liberating story. But it also allows us to see ourselves in liberating and vocation-centered relationships through our imaginative engagement in the role of the helpers in the story. Moreover, it fosters re-imaging our relationship with God through Jesus Christ and the liberation and vocation that is energized in that relationship.

ACTIVITY 1—*Disclose the Bible Story/Text*

I invite persons to enter the story of the paralytic found in Mark 2:1-12. I introduce the Scripture as a story about a man who was paralyzed and that the paralysis was an impediment to his ability to live a full life. But he experienced a life-changing event. I then indicate that we will have three readings of the story. The first reading takes place in this first activity. This reading, guided by the following questions, is done individually and silently.

* Within what kind of group did the story take place?
* Where was the paralytic in relation to the group in the beginning of the story?
* How did his position in relation to the group change as the story progressed? Why?
* What were the four helpers' roles, behaviors, and attitudes?
* What was the role, behavior, and attitude of the paralytic?
* How essential was Jesus to the unfolding story and why?
* What role did the Pharisees and the crowd play?
* What conclusions can be drawn about liberating and vocation-centered relationships, about a "we" orientation to handling troubling life events, and about celebration?

Responses to the questions are addressed in Activity 2.

ACTIVITY 2—*Focus on the Bible Story as Mirror*

Participants respond within the whole group setting to the guiding questions posed in activity 1. To assist this response, the questions are repeated.

Reflection Exercise. Read the story of the paralytic found in Mark 2:1-12. Consider your answers to the questions raised above.

Some responses given by actual participants are as follows:

"The group had already assembled before the paralytic arrived. There was a possibility that the paralytic was going to be left out. The crowd would probably have been oblivious to the paralytic's absence. As the paralytic was brought forward by the four helpers, the crowd apparently put up some resistance. Extraordinary means had to be made for him to be included."

"The paralytic relied on the four helpers to get him to a point of transformation. He also believed that his paralysis did not have to continue. Liberation was not based solely on individual effort. It was a community effort. There was definitely 'we'-oriented effort. And the helpers were definitely exercising vocation."

"The crowd was moved by what took place. Their response might be called a kind of celebration. The Pharisees gave what was called 'bad press.' But they weren't obstructive."

"Jesus was the true source of the transforming event. The actions of the helpers and the paralytic were generated by their awareness of the presence of Jesus. Liberating relationships, showing caring that is at the center of vocation, and being inspired by and having a relationship with Jesus are all interrelated."

ACTIVITY 3—*Enter as Partner with Bible Story Actors*

In activity 3, participants engage in two dramatized readings or actual role-plays of the story of the paralytic. I invite participants to identify with or to take on the role of the paralytic during the first dramatized reading. They identify with the helpers in the final reading of the Scripture. I encourage persons to get in touch with what is happening to them as they take on the roles of the paralytic and the helpers. They note their relationships with others in the story and with Jesus. Participants' attention to their feelings about themselves and what happens to them as they "live" the story is also encouraged.

The dramatized readings require a prewritten script and the assignment of parts to various participants. The parts include two narrators, the paralytic, Jesus, three Pharisees, and the crowd. The story parts are as follows.

Narrator 1: When he (Jesus) was returned to Capernaum after some days, it was reported that he was at home. So many gathered around that there was no longer room for them, not even in front of the door; and he was speaking the word to them.

Narrator 2: Then some people came, bringing to him a paralyzed man, carried by four of them. And when they could not bring him to Jesus because of the crowd, they removed the roof about him; and after having dug through it, they let down the mat on which the paralytic lay.

Narrator 1: When Jesus saw their faith, he said to the paralytic:

Jesus: Son, your sins are forgiven.

Narrator 1: Now some of the scribes were sitting there, questioning in their hearts,

The Three Pharisees: Why does this fellow speak in this way? It is blasphemy! Who can forgive sins but God alone?

Narrator 2: At once Jesus perceived in his spirit that they were discussing these questions among themselves; and he said to them,

Jesus: Why do you raise such questions in your hearts? Which is easier to say to the paralytic, "Your sins are forgiven," or to say, "Stand up and take your mat and walk"? But so that you may know that the Son of Man has authority on earth to forgive sins . . .

Narrator 1: He said to the paralytic,

Jesus: I say to you, stand up, take your mat and go to your home.

Narrator 2: And he stood up, and immediately took the mat and went out before all of them; so they were all amazed and glorified God saying,

Crowd: We have never seen anything like this!

At the close of each of the two dramatized readings, participants respond to the guiding question: What feelings did the role playing evoke in you?

Reflection Exercise. Image yourself as the paralytic in the story. Then image yourself as one of the helpers. Based on your imaging, respond to the above question.

Some responses given by actual participants are as follows:

"As the paralytic, I felt like an outcast, embarrassed, angry, and helpless in the beginning. The helpers gave me a new feeling of strength. Their willingness to help me gave me a new lease on life. Somebody cared! I knew the moment they lifted me up that I was going to be included with everybody else. I felt like the crowd was looking at me and thinking, 'What right do you have to intrude and make a grand entrance?' But the helpers made me see that I did have a right. And, they got me included the only way they could."

"The presence of Jesus was powerful to me. The nearer I got to him, the more I felt empowered. Knowing I was in his presence and he in mine dispelled my feelings of being an outcast. I was no longer embarrassed, angry, or helpless. I was enabled to move back through the crowd on my own. I went back home whole."

"As a helper, I felt the weight of the paralytic. It was more the weight of responsibility for the paralytic. With the weight and all, I knew I could get to a point where I would simply drop the paralytic and maybe have a hard time helping him up again. I felt this especially while moving through the crowd."

"I felt myself struggling trying not to let the crowd overtake me or discourage my efforts."

ACTIVITY 4—*Envision God's Activity Today*

Activity 4 helps identify where God is at work among African Americans today. How is God bringing about liberating and vocation-oriented relationships?

I invite participants to choose partners. With their partners, they recall one specific person whom they feel God sent to care for them. They recall the name of the person, what the person looks like, and their relationship to the person. They recall when and how the person showed caring. And they recall how they felt about this relationship.

I also invite participants to recall in the presence of their partners an instance when they felt God called them to be positive and caring helpers for another person. They recall the name of the person, what the person looks like, and their relationship to the person. They recall the circumstance under which they felt called to help. And they recall how they felt about this relationship.

Participants are then invited to recall an instance when they felt God worked through the church or other institutions to bring justice and harmony in the midst of injustice and turmoil. They recall the circumstances requiring action, who was involved, and how the church or others responded. The partners conclude this activity with one or both partners offering a prayer of gratitude for God's presence through caring relationships.

Reflection Exercise. Reflect on your own story of relationships using the above format.

ACTIVITY 5—*Anticipate Ongoing Response to God*

In this period of sharing, two sets of partners combine to identify where God is now calling for caring responses. Particular attention is given to troubling or paralyzing relationships and life events among African Americans. We call to mind events and specific troubling relationships about which we are aware in families, work, school, church, community, and other places. We then list them on newsprint or tablet for use in the final phase of the story-linking process. Examples of responses on newsprint or tablet have typically included:

Family: Difficulty caring for an elderly parent whose health is declining and who resists help.
Work: Experience of job layoff, insufficient benefits, and inability in finding other employment.
School: Increasing violence, negative regard and racist comments by white teachers toward African Americans.
Church: An "in-group" attitude makes newcomers feel unwelcome.
Community: Animosity between African American residents and non–African American neighborhood store owners.

Reflection Exercise. What troubling or paralyzing relationships and life events are in need of caring response in your community?

PHASE THREE: *Engaging Christian Faith Stories from African American Heritage*

How did our forebears confront troubling or paralyzing relationships and life events? An important story to illustrate this phase of the story-linking process is that of Josiah Henson.[1] It tells of a man and his family who experienced the solidarity of family amidst the brutality of slavery. In this story, we become privy to the enlivening presence of God in the lives of persons whose relationships and life events would be considered by most to be dead-end. We discover a man who saw a "we" orientation as the only way to show Christian caring.

ACTIVITY 1—*Disclose the Faith Heritage Story*

I invite persons to glean as much as they can about the nature of relationships and life events, and how they are dealt with in the Josiah Henson story. The story may be presented on prerecorded audiotape using one African American voice for the narrator portions. An African American male voice should be used where Henson's first person words appear. An African American female's voice should be used where Mother Henson's words appear. Participants may also present the story as indicated below:

Narrator: Josiah Henson was born a slave in 1789. His first recollection was of his father's severe beating because his father had come to the defense of Josiah's mother who was being accosted by the slave overseer. Josiah described seeing the penalty being meted out.

Josiah: The penalty was one hundred lashes on his bare back, and his right ear nailed to the whipping-post, and then severed from his body.

Narrator: Josiah's father was later sent from the state of Maryland (where this happened) to Alabama. Josiah's mother and six children remained on the estate. He thought of her:

Josiah: She was a good mother to us, a woman of deep piety, anxious above all things to touch our hearts with a sense of religion. I don't know how or where she acquired her acquaintance with the Lord's Prayer, which she so frequently taught us to repeat. . . . I remember seeing her often on her knees, trying to arrange her thoughts in prayer appropriate to her situation, . . . and which have remained in my memory to this hour. . . . We were but property—not a mother and children God had given her.

85

Narrator: And Josiah remembered that because of the reality that they were property, the children were eventually sold, one by one, away from their mother and then she was sold. Josiah was about five or six years old when this happened. He recalled his mother pleading for her children only to be kicked away.

Josiah: I saw the groan of her suffering body and the sob of her breaking heart. I heard her cry out:

Mother: Oh, Lord Jesus, how long, how long shall I suffer this way?

Narrator: Throughout his early years as a slave, Josiah was oppressed by his circumstances and oppressed "with a load of sorrow" for the male slaves' condition which was bad enough, but more particularly for the slave women's suffering. He felt driven to do whatever he could for them in a clandestine way.

At eighteen years old, Josiah came to believe that he had a responsibility to God. He had sneaked away to hear a sermon at the risk of being caught and beaten. He heard the scriptural passage of Hebrews 2:19, which told that God, through Christ, tasted death for *everyone.* For the first time, he felt the confirmation of a Supreme Being who had compassion for *all,* including him and others living under the sting of oppression. Josiah found himself saying:

Josiah: Jesus will be my dear refuge—he'll wipe away all tears from my eyes. Now I can bear all things; nothing will seem hard after this.

Narrator: He described this as his conversion, or the awakening of a new life—a consciousness of a new power and destiny.

Josiah's suffering in the throes of slavery continued, but he also continued to do whatever he could for others who shared the same miserable condition. He married a slave girl. They had twelve children, eight of whom survived childhood. He admits to acting out of ignorance on some occasions. He did not apologize for his feeling of hatred of the system and bitterness toward those in the system who often promised one thing and did another. He became absorbed with the quest for his soul for freedom and self-assertion. For he said:

Josiah: I am ready and willing to pray and to put forth vigorous action.

Narrator: At one point Josiah gained his freedom and a certificate showing it only to find himself tricked out of them and pushed to be wholly reliant on God. At another point, he was taken away from his wife and children.

Josiah: I was placed in a "slave-pen." I felt sure I'd die.

Narrator: Josiah contemplated murder as a means of insuring his escape. But he could not go through with it. He said:

Josiah: To murder would destroy my own character, the value of life and my peace of mind.

Narrator: Still, he was reunited with his wife and two children, and together, they were able to escape to freedom. They reached Cincinnati, Ohio, and were able to get the comfort of rest and shelter from good Samaritans. After resting, they headed on through the wilderness. They happened onto an Indian encampment and received hospitality from the Indians. They finally knew they were delivered when they were picked up by a boat. This was in 1830. Josiah described it:

Josiah: My black friend and two sailors jumped out. . . . Three hearty cheers welcomed us as we reached the schooner, and never till my dying shall I forget the shout of the captain: "Come up on deck and clap your wings and crow like a rooster. You're free."

Narrator: You can imagine Josiah's joy.

Josiah: I threw myself on the ground, rolled in the sand, seized handfuls of it and kissed them, and danced round till, in the eyes of several who were present, I passed for a madman.

Narrator: Josiah became a preacher. As his eldest boy learned to read in school, he taught Josiah to read. Josiah saw that there was room for betterment in the conditions of the blacks in the place where they settled. He also felt that none of them should be content with the first joy of their deliverance. Josiah insisted that they needed to become of one mind for their betterment.

And Josiah himself felt called to work for the liberation of brothers and sisters still in slavery. He said:

Josiah: After I had tasted the blessings of freedom, my mind reverted to those whom I knew were groaning in captivity, and I at once proceeded to take measures to free as many as I could. I thought that, by using exertion, numbers might make their escape as I did, if they had some practical advice how to proceed.

Narrator: Moreover, in his preaching Josiah tried to impress upon other blacks who had tasted freedom something else about their obligations. He said:

Josiah: We are obligated first to God, for our deliverance; and then, second, to our fellow sojourners, to do all that is in our power to bring others out of bondage.

ACTIVITY 2—*Describe the Liberation Mind-set and Liberation and Vocational Strategies*

Participants share their observations of relationships, life events, and how these were dealt with in the story. In particular, group members are asked to look for a communal liberation mind-set in the story and for a "we" strategy in addressing paralyzing life events. The guiding questions are:

* What evidence did you see of Josiah Henson's unwavering focus on liberation for him, his family, and others?
* Why didn't he give up? Where in his story did a "we" strategy appear?
* How would you compare his story to the story of the paralytic found in the Gospel of Mark?
* What qualities in the Josiah Henson story would you like to emulate?
* What qualities would you like to see emulated in your church community?

Reflection Exercise. What answers would you give to the questions? Responses of actual participants include:

"The family unit was important to Josiah and freedom for all of them, not just for himself, was pivotal. But it was clear that he had a commitment to the liberation of 'fellow sojourners.' In these ways his strategy was definitely 'we' oriented."

"He had a real relationship with God and that relationship propelled him forward to help others no matter what. He had reverence for the life of all. He chose to take the opportunities that came as he saw them rather than to murder."

"Our churches—each one of us—need the communal commitment that Josiah had. We also need to be willing to admit, as he did, that we don't always have the answers and we may make some ignorant moves along the way. Yet, together, we can make it."

PHASE FOUR: *Engaging in Christian Ethical Decision Making*

The intent in the final phase of the story-linking process is to guide persons toward deciding action. We give particular attention to what God is calling us to do to respond to troubling relationships the groups listed earlier on newsprint or tablets. We are also to decide ways to celebrate positive relations and events.

ACTIVITY 1—*Discern God's Call*

The groups begin by reviewing the list of troubling relationships and events they listed on the newsprint or tablet in phase two. The groups are then invited to engage in a "silent memory summation" of the story of the paralytic and the Josiah Henson story. In this summation exercise, group members call to mind two or three relational qualities in the stories that struck them as being important to a communal mind-set. These qualities become a starting point for the groups' describing the kind of communal mind-set needed to address the troubling or paralyzing relationships and life events they listed earlier on newsprint. Participants are guided by the question, What are the qualities—including attitudes, ideas, and approaches—needed to carry out caring responses to troubling relationships and events in each participant's family, work, school, church, and community?

Reflection Exercise. Take some time for your silent memory summation. Then describe your communal mind-set.
Responses of actual participants include:

"Imagining the presence of Jesus, communal prayer, loss of fear, verbalized willingness to reach out are ways of being communal."

"Taking the time to show caring and making a commitment to give back to community are at the center of a communal mind-set."

"Not leaving others behind, but at the same time acknowledging when we need help and seeking to help one another is important."

ACTIVITY 2—*Decide Concrete Actions*

In the final activity, persons decide how and when to respond to God's call to address troubling or paralyzing relationships and life events. From the newsprint or tablet list, the group designates one relationship or life event as highest priority. The groups brainstorm all possible actions they and their church can take that hold realistic potential for positive response. From the options, they choose one action for themselves and one for the church. They then develop specific approaches and a time line to accomplish the actions. Examples of suggested actions include the following:

* Form a "You and Your Aging Parent" workshop with leaders who can provide advice on caring for aging relatives.
* Create a job bank with lists of available jobs in the community and persons who can assist in application and interview preparation.
* Initiate an "Adopt a School" program in the church.
* Hold an open church forum on what it means to be a welcoming church. Volunteer to be greeters for new visitors to church services.
* Establish meetings between African American community residents and leaders and non–African American neighborhood

store owners to forge working relationships and to air grievances in helpful ways.

Finally, the groups decide a way of celebrating their group relationship that can be used in other places. Ideas include writing a litany or poem, celebrating through song and/or movement, developing a "Welcome Table" communion service. The small groups then share their decisions with the whole group.

Follow-up Suggestions

Develop your own everyday case studies on interpersonal relationships and life events or ask group participants to do so. The following alternative Bible passages may be used in follow-up sessions: Psalm 13; Psalm 33:13-22; and Romans 12:9-13, 13:8-10. For persons who are presently struggling with difficult relationships and life events, Psalm 13 offers an avenue for voicing and reflecting openly on anguish. This Psalm should be presented, however, with Psalm 33:13-22. The latter text allows persons to identify with the theme of promise. The passage from Romans is helpful because of its focus on qualities that characterize liberating and vocation-centered relationships. Also, central to this passage is a "we" orientation.

An alternate African American Christian faith heritage story that also depicts liberating and vocation-centered relationships and a "we" orientation is that of Irene McCoy Gaines. Out of her struggles as an African American woman, Ms. Gaines became a civil rights activist, civic worker, social worker, and advocate on behalf of African Americans. Her story is found in *Notable Black American Women,* edited by Jessie Carney Smith.[2]

Sermon material may also be substituted in the heritage story phase. For example, the sermon by H. Beecher Hicks, Jr. entitled "I've Been in the Storm So Long," found in *Preaching Through a Storm,* addresses the theme of triumph out of anguish.[3]

Exploring
Life Meanings Through
Story-Linking

It is ever a grace and a benediction to be able to come to a halt . . . to turn aside from the things that occupy and preoccupy our minds in the daily round, to take a long intimate look at ourselves both retrospect and prospect . . . It is at such times that we are free to remember! From within the quiet of our spirits we may see with startling clarity the meaning of past experiences.

—HOWARD THURMAN
THE INWARD JOURNEY

Assigning meaning to our experiences is a natural and important way of making sense of life. In meaning-making, we ponder and judge all that makes up our lives—our self-identities, social contexts, interpersonal relationships, and life events. Our meaning-making is our attempt to bring order and purpose in our lives. Meaning-making is our way of saying, "This is how I see life and my place in it, and this is what I'm going to do about it." How we fill in and act on the details contributes to our story plot. And how our story plot unfolds contributes to our ongoing meaning-making. So, life meanings and story plots are very much related.

We assign meanings to the happenings of our lives and arrive at various degrees of understandings of our purposes, and we have a great deal to say about how our plots unfold. Indeed, we have a lot to say about whether our unfolding plots will be liberating or blocking for us and others and whether they do or do not reflect our being in vocation. How is this so? Our plot is defined by an undergirding theme in our lives. This theme is our dominant approach to life. How we act on our approach to life forms our purpose or the direction we choose to go in life. This contributes to the character of our unfolding plot.

When we become Christians, we choose a Christian story plot. We see life through the eyes of God made known in Jesus Christ. Our being in life is seen as a gift, as valuable, and as having promise even in the midst of trials and tribulations. We choose to be linked with and set our life direction after the Example and Source of a liberating plot. Our unfolding plot becomes defined by hope-filled purpose, based on God's ongoing value of us and expectation of our valuing others. It becomes defined by care and concern that extends beyond self to others. We see our purpose in vocational terms and as a calling from God.

But, someone is apt to say, "Hold it! Not so fast! It's not that easy!" And we know these thoughts sometimes come. When we are assailed by ongoing racial discrimination and other trials and tribulations, there is the temptation to succumb to an approach to life that says, "Life is a horrid mistake." Or "Life is a barrel of lemons out of which no lemonade can possibly be made." But the nature of vocation as calling demands that we find and choose those ways wherein Christ becomes present through each one of us. We choose to continue to reach out, hold, sustain, and advocate on behalf of one another until any block to liberation for us and others is dismantled. How is this possible?

In this chapter, we will engage in a story-linking process focused on life meanings and story plots. Our intent is to become critically aware of both. We will consider whether our story plots are liberating and whether they contain a sense of vocation and positive life meaning from the Christian viewpoint. Likewise, we will consider hindrances to living the Christian story plot and arriving at positive life meanings based on this plot. We want to become alert to judgments we have of our stories as dissatisfying, futile, or meaningless; and we want to determine what is needed to reorient such stories toward positive life meanings. The case studies of Mary Johnson and Ken Brown will continue as means of entering the story-linking process focused on life meanings.

PHASE ONE: *Engaging the Everyday Story*

The following case material reveals aspects of Mary's and Ken's self-identity, social contexts, interpersonal relationships, and life events. However, we focus expressly on meanings Mary and Ken assigned to their lives and on the nature of their story plots.

CASE STUDY 1: *Mary Johnson's Story*

In continuing her story, Mary Johnson was quick to say:

"My life has been no bed of roses. But I'd guess you could say that about most, if not all, of us. Do you know anyone who has lived a perfect trouble-free life? I surely don't, although I'm sure some have had a worse time of it than I, judging from what I know about real hardship cases—abuse, you name it—in the school where I teach. Sometimes, it's hard to be optimistic about life, but I do look at myself pretty much as an optimist. Basically, I believe you can't give up on life. If you're going to get anything out of life, somehow you're going to have to hang in there. Still, I confess there have been times when I was guilty of throwing my hands up and, for a time, sitting down on life.

"I recall when my husband, my children, and I moved because of my husband's job transfer. I was not what you'd call happy. I wasn't working. My husband and I got into some marital conflict. I gained a lot of weight. And to top it off, the church I thought was going to be supportive and active did not turn out to be that way. It didn't turn out to be a welcoming place and the attitudes there left me feeling alienated. With all that happened, my life just stalled.

"I remember thinking that I was doomed. I couldn't seem to get motivated to start teaching again. And, frankly, I questioned what I had to contribute. My children were all that held me together. I became a totally dependent person with no life of my own and no financial resources of my own. I hit bottom.

"I remember going to a New Year's Eve service at a church other than the one I joined. The sermon was on 'Christian Responsibility for a New Day.' During the last part of the service, those attending were asked to write a letter to God about how we felt about our lives. We were to confess to God what we had not done for ourselves and others that we could and should have done as responsible Christians. We were to tell God what we intended to do in the New Year. And we were to ask for and cooperate with God's guidance.

"Now, I am not one for New Year's resolutions. But I saw this letter differently. I found myself pouring out to God all I could in the time we had to write the letter—my inadequate feelings, my feelings that my life had gone 'down the drain,' my disappointment in myself and in my church. I wrote that I was going to live my life differently in the New Year. I admitted that I had abilities I had laid aside. I wrote that I would seek certification for teaching. I also said that I would not keep quiet about the church's alienating atmosphere since I knew it was affecting others. And I committed to daily prayer. When we finished, we were told to put the letters in an envelope we had been given. We sealed the envelopes, addressed them to ourselves, and placed them at the altar during communion. We were told the envelopes would be mailed to us at year's end.

"Over the year, I found myself being guided and empowered by God. I enrolled in school to get teacher certification. I applied for and got a position as a teaching assistant. I spoke to church leaders about the alienating atmosphere, and it became an important item for discussion and action. I faithfully prayed every day. My life definitely moved in a different direction. Hopefully, I'm helping somebody. For me, that's what it's all about. Anyway, I got the letter back at the end of the year. I saw how important it is not to give up on life. Plus, I found it's important not to give up on myself. Don't get me wrong. Life still is no bed of roses. But God gives us a new chance every day. As long as I have this chance, I have hope. That's the bottom line. That's what helps me to be optimistic."

CASE STUDY 2: *Ken Brown's Story*

Ken continued his story by saying:

"It is difficult to think of my life without thinking about the lives of those I grew up with and where I grew up—my brothers and sisters, neighbors, dilapidated apartments and houses, tight spaces, not much to live on, gangs, drugs. You see, I was able somehow to find my way out. But for most of the others, nothing has changed except a new generation growing up in the same place in the same way. I'll have to admit, a big part of me—my heart—is still there. When I think of all that needs to be done in that place and in places like it all over the country. . . . (Ken's voice trailed off.)

"So, when I think about meaning in life, it's hard for me to separate meaning as far as I'm concerned and meaning as far as those I grew up with are concerned. Yes, I've heard people say life is what you make it, and there's some truth in that. But people get to where they are for many reasons. Some by their own doing, some because of tough breaks in life, and some because they were born into it. But I have seen what the conditions of poor people can do to you. My mother and many others like her had a lot of pride. She and a lot of others did everything they could that's honest and decent to make a decent life where, in a lot of ways, there was little that made for real living in terms of the things they needed to survive. I know that hasn't changed for a whole lot of folk. It's often a real fight for them to hold their heads up.

"Many outside the neighborhood were frankly unfriendly, insensitive and discouraging. I told you earlier about the unkind paramedics. That is only the tip of the iceberg, when it comes to how people in our neighborhood are treated by public agencies and officials who are supposed to care. Churches are not always that much different either. Also, slumlords are for real. There's only so much that you can fix up or patch up. After a while, people just give up. You've heard that old saying, 'You can't fight city hall.' Well, when you're poor, you feel like for sure you can't, so what happens is that a lot of 'kicking one another' goes on inside the neighborhood. It's a way of kicking at whatever reminds you of your own inadequacy, inferiority, and humiliation. Even though it's not a good way to deal with the raw deals life gives you, it happens nonetheless. When people feel defeated, well. . . . (Ken's voice trailed off.)

"I ran across a book one time called *Growing Up Absurd* [by Paul Goodman] that said that when people do not see anything worthwhile, they cannot do anything worthwhile. They begin to feel like their lives are starved. And when their lives are starved, they begin to ask the question, 'Am I nothing?' That's what life means to a lot of people I know. I know that's the case with the homeless people who come to the soup kitchen where I currently volunteer. It's the case with some youth I am working with. That has to change. In order for my life to have meaning, I feel I've got to do something to help change things. I know that's what I've been called to do."

ACTIVITY 1—*Disclose the Everyday Story*

As suggested previously, the case study material may be presented through prerecorded audiotape using African American voices. Or it may be read aloud by participants—a female for Mary's story and a male for Ken's story. Or the material may be read aloud to the participants by the leader(s)/teacher(s).

In an actual Christian education setting, I invite persons in advance of the case disclosures to listen with the following questions in mind:

* Do Mary and Ken link with a liberating plot and, if so, what is that plot?
* Do Mary and Ken have an overall sense of purpose in life that is liberating for them and is potentially liberating for others? How do you know?
* Is there anything in their stories that conveys that they have dealt with positive and negative meanings in life? If so, where and how did they do it?
* How do you feel about Mary's and Ken's views about life and what issues do their stories raise for you?

ACTIVITY 2—*Critically Reflect on the Case Material*

I repeat the questions raised prior to the case disclosures and invite participants to share their responses.

Reflection Exercise. What answers would you give to the questions posed above?

The following are responses given by actual participants:

Reflections on Mary Johnson's Meaning-Making

"Mary says she looks at life optimistically. That's the main theme or plot to her story. But she also seems to look at life realistically. Life isn't a bed of roses. Life is hard. But given that reality, Mary doesn't stay down when she gets down. That's a plus in terms of making any kind of sense and meaning out of life."

"She's also a risk-taker. She went to another church and responded to something she saw as useful. It sounds like she went looking for her liberation and vocation. She went back to her own church to 'blow the whistle.' That took courage and by doing what she did, she helped free them to a better kind of vocation. Plus it made her feel better about her own life."

"Her story put us on notice that meaning in life doesn't come by sitting still. People can't sit still and let life run over them if they expect to contribute something to life and get something out of life."

"Mary also showed that you can get energized when you're in touch with God. She showed that Christians can find purpose and exercise purpose when they're in touch with God. That's the only way to make sense out of life."

"Mary's on track in terms of vocation. She stopped resisting her calling to teach. But her story raises the issue for a lot of people, including some of us, that we do resist what God is calling us to do and then we wonder why we have a problem with meaning in life."

Reflections on Ken Brown's Meaning-Making

"When you have a hard life like Ken's, it's a hard thing seeing things positively. But Ken is able to do that. However, the main theme or story plot is seeing himself in others, not forgetting where he came from, having hope, and getting involved. He doesn't find real meaning in his life unless he gets involved with people who have a precarious hope but who are looking for and needing liberation of every type imaginable. What he says about meaning for himself reminds us of the 'we' orientation we learned about earlier."

"Ken sure hits us with our responsibility to minister to others so that they can find hope and positive meaning in their lives. Really, he's convicted many of us. On the other hand, how far can we go in taking responsibility? Yet, when we look at Ken's brothers and sisters, how much can Ken or we do for someone who doesn't seem to want help or doesn't seem to help themselves? Questions about how hard to try plus not knowing exactly what to do can block our vocation, their liberation and our meaning in life. At the same time, we ought not use that as an excuse to cop out of our responsibility to be in vocation, because if we do, we've failed our calling to vocation."

"Ken is certainly not copping out. He said he's *got* to do something. For him, it's a mandate—his calling. He definitely got a vision of what he *had to do* from God. And, as far as that is concerned, it seems like he won't be satisfied with his life until he makes good on it with others. He's challenged us."

ACTIVITY 3—*Identify with the Case Study*

Following critical reflection on the case studies, I invite participants to share with a partner or in small groups what the case material evoked in them about their own meaning-making. Starter questions include:

* To what extent did you see your own plot or generating theme in Mary's and Ken's stories?

* Is the way you look at life and go about life similar to or different from Mary and Ken? How?
* What impact does life outlook have on your sense of being liberated and being in vocation? What impact does it have on life meaning for you?
* What words or phrases would you use to describe the plot or generating theme of your story?

Responses to the questions are then shared in the large group.

Reflection Exercise. Reflect on your life meaning in light of Mary's and Ken's story. How would you answer the questions?

I have found that some persons more closely identify with what Mary had to say than to Ken's statements—while, for others, it is just the reverse. There are also those who say that what Mary or Ken shared could very well have been their own story. In comparing their own stories with Mary's and Ken's, some persons find clear points of differentiation. Others are more apt to share the difficulties they have in coming to positive life meaning. It is important that the leader/teacher guides the group to avoid "getting stuck" at this point. This may be done by encouraging them to stay with the story-linking process and to see what the rest of the process has to say to them.

PHASE TWO: *Engaging the Christian Faith Story in the Bible*

In phase two, we link our reflections on Mary's, Ken's, and our stories with Scripture. The question is: What does Scripture have to say about life meaning? The following illustrates an approach to answering the question.

A helpful passage is Hebrews 10:39, 11:1-40, 12:1-2. This particular passage is helpful to an African American discussion of life meaning because it reveals a message about the meaning of life amidst adversity and oppression on which African Americans, past and present, have relied. In fact, in African American church settings, the "Honor Roll of the Faithful," which appears in chapter 11 of Hebrews, is often appended to include an Honor Roll of African Americans who have kept the faith.

In the passage from Hebrews, we find faith as the major theme. The author was responding to early Christians who were discouraged and had lost hope and meaning due to the perils of life, harassment, and oppression. The Scripture witnesses to what it means to seek, find, and refuse to relinquish faith that brings positive life meaning in the midst of trials and tribulations.

The Scripture provides for African Americans a litany of God's relationship with another people. It evokes our telling of God's acting in our own history. It reveals a perspective of faith and hope in God's ongoing relationship with us and God's desire for our liberation, vocation, and life meaning. Indeed, it challenges us to reflect on our faith in God's activity, on our response to God's Word in whatever situation we find ourselves today, and on the relation of these to our meaning-making.

ACTIVITY 1—*Disclose the Bible Story*

I invite persons to enter the passage from Hebrews. I introduce the Scripture by saying that it tells the story of a writer's response to early Christians who lived in a place called the Lycus Valley. They were discouraged and confronted doubts and hopelessness due to adversity and oppression. Participants are then invited into two readings of the Scripture. First, they read the passage alone silently, or they read the verses alternately with a partner. Second, the whole group enters into a choral reading of the Scripture.

In advance of the choral reading, I provide questions to consider, including:

* What was the plot or generating theme in the Scripture? What words or phrases convey the plot? Would you describe the plot as liberating? Why?
* Would you say that those on the "Honor Roll of Faith" were in vocation? Why? What meanings did life have for them?
* In what ways does the Scripture challenge your approach to life and meaning-making today?

It is helpful to explain that a choral reading involves solo and unison recitations of Scripture. Through it, we create drama by blending words and sentences together in much the same way as an orchestra blends instruments. Before assigning parts, it is also helpful to explain difficult words and work on their pronunciation. Three soloists, two choruses, and all are needed as follows:

All: We are not among those who shrink back and so are lost, but among those who have faith and so are saved.

Solo 1: Now faith is the assurance of things hoped for, the conviction of things not seen. Indeed by faith our ancestors received approval.

All: By faith we understand that the worlds were prepared by the word of God, so that what is seen was made from things that are not visible.

Chorus 1: By faith Abel offered to God a more acceptable sacrifice than Cain's. Through this he received approval as righteous, God himself giving approval to his gifts; he died, but through his faith he still speaks.

Chorus 2: By faith Enoch was taken so that he did not experience death; and "he was not found, because God had taken him." For it was attested before he was taken away that "he had pleased God."

Solo 2: And without faith it is impossible to please God, for whoever would approach him must believe that he exists and that he rewards those who seek him.

Chorus 1: By faith Noah, warned by God about events as yet unseen, respected the warning and built an ark to save his household; by this he condemned the world and became an heir to the righteousness that is in accordance with faith.

Chorus 2: By faith Abraham obeyed when he was called to set out for a place that he was to receive as an inheritance; and he set out not knowing where he was going. By faith he stayed for a time in the land he had been promised, as in a foreign land, living in tents, as did Isaac and Jacob, who were heirs with him of the same promise. For he looked forward to the city that has foundations, whose architect and builder is God.

Chorus 1: By faith he received power of procreation, even though he was too old—and Sarah herself was barren—because he considered him faithful who had promised. Therefore from one person, and this one as good as dead, descendants were born, "as many as the stars of heaven and as the innumerable grains of sand by the seashore."

Solo 3: All of these died in faith without having received the promises, but from a distance they saw and greeted them.

Solo 1: They confessed that they were strangers and foreigners on the earth, for people who speak in this way make it clear that they are seeking a homeland.

Solo 2: If they had been thinking of the land that they had left behind, they would have had opportunity to return. But, as it is, they desire a better country, that is, a heavenly one.

All soloists: Therefore, God is not ashamed to be called their God; indeed, he has prepared a city for them.

Chorus 1: By faith Abraham, when put to the test, offered up Isaac. He who had received the promises was ready to offer up his only son, of whom he had been told,

Solo 3: "It is through Isaac that descendants shall be named for you."

Chorus 1: He considered the fact that God is able even to raise someone from the dead—and figuratively speaking, he did receive him back.

Chorus 2: By faith Jacob, when dying, blessed each of the sons of Joseph, "bowing in worship over the top of his staff."

Chorus 1: By faith Joseph, at the end of his life, made mention of the Exodus of the Israelites and gave instructions about his burial.

Solo 1: By faith Moses was hidden by his parents for three months after his birth, because they saw that the child was beautiful, and they were not afraid of the king's edict.

Solo 2: By faith, Moses, when he was grown up, refused to be called a son of Pharaoh's daughter, choosing rather to share ill-treatment with the people of God than to enjoy the fleeting pleasures of sin.

Solo 3: He considered abuse suffered for God to be greater wealth than the treasures of Egypt, for he was looking ahead to the reward.

Solo 1: By faith he left Egypt, unafraid of the King's anger; for he persevered as though he saw him who is invisible.

Solo 2: By faith he kept the Passover and the sprinkling of blood, so that the destroyer of the firstborn would not touch the first-born of Israel.

Chorus 1: By faith the people passed through the Red Sea as if it were dry land, but when the Egyptians attempted to do so they were drowned.

Chorus 2: By faith the walls of Jericho fell after they had been encircled for seven days.

Chorus 1: By faith Rahab the prostitute did not perish with those who were disobedient, because she had received the spies in peace.

Solo 3: And what more should I say? For time would fail me to tell of Gideon, Barak, Samson, Jephthah, of David and Samuel and the prophets—who through faith conquered kingdoms, administered justice, obtained promises, shut the mouths of lions, quenched raging fire, escaped the edge of the sword, won strength out of weakness, became mighty in war, put foreign armies to flight.

Solo 1: Women received their dead by resurrection. Others were tortured, refusing to accept release, in order to obtain a better resurrection.

Solo 2: Others suffered mocking and flogging, and even chains and imprisonment. They were stoned to death; they were sawn in two; they were killed by the sword; they went about in skins of sheep and goats, destitute, persecuted, tormented—of whom the world was not worthy. They wandered in deserts and mountains, and in caves and holes in the ground.

Chorus 1: Yet, all these, though they were commended for their faith, did not receive what was promised, since God had provided something better so that they would not, apart from us, be made perfect.

All: Therefore, since we are surrounded by so great a cloud of witnesses, let us also lay aside every weight and the sin that clings so closely, and let us run with perseverance the race that is set before us, looking to Jesus the pioneer and perfecter of our faith, who for the sake of the joy that was set before him endured the cross, disregarding its shame, and has taken his seat at the right hand of the throne of God.

ACTIVITY 2—*Focus on the Bible Story as Mirror*

In activity 2 we approach the passage from Hebrews as a mirror for looking at life meanings in Mary's, Ken's, and our own stories. Because of our participation in the church and the importance of the church's role in our lives and meaning-making, we will also look at our church's story plot and meaning-making. To enter this activity, I present again the questions raised prior to the choral reading. Participants are then invited to share responses to the questions either in the whole group setting or in small groups.

Reflection Exercise. Reflect on the Scripture and consider your responses to the questions raised in the preceding section.

Some responses of actual participants are as follows:

"The main theme or plot is faith in spite of all the stuff that the people in the story faced. People on the honor roll of faith knew that you can't get positive meaning out of life if you don't believe in something larger than life and bigger than yourself. They knew who that was—God. Granted, it's hard to keep the faith sometimes, but you can see others did it. *Faith* is the *big word* in the plot. It's like in the song we sing, 'God Didn't Bring Me This Far to Leave Me.' "

SOUL STORIES

"Another *big word* that defined the plot is *obedience* to God. The people on the honor roll of faith knew that you can't get positive meaning out of life if you're not willing to live like God wants you to live. They didn't just live for themselves. They lived and did what they did with others in mind. They heard what God wanted for their lives, and they responded. They were in vocation. It's like they knew the gospel song, 'I'm Gonna Live the Life God Wants Me to Live.'"

"*Perseverance* is also a *big word* in the plot. The people on the honor roll of faith knew that you can't get positive meaning out of life unless you 'keep on keeping on' in life's journey in spite of all the negatives in life. It's like they were living out the spirituals, 'Hold On Just a Little Bit Longer, Everything's Gonna Be Alright,' and 'Keep Hold of God's Unchanging Hand.'"

ACTIVITY 3—*Enter as Partner with Bible Story Actors*

I invite participants to sing songs that they connected to the Scripture or I select a revered song like those mentioned above. I then invite them to choose one of the persons on the "Honor Roll of Faith" with which they identify. Those who choose the same person on the "Honor Roll" form a group. Prewritten depictions of the persons is given to each participant or group. They preview the depiction and determine one or more ways it reflects their own story plot and struggle for life meaning. After this, participants share the depictions and their responses with the whole group. To illustrate, six first-person depictions are provided below.[1]

Noah. I am Noah, the son of Lamech, the grandson of Methuselah, and the ninth descendant from Adam. At one point in my life, God directed me to do what seemed to be the impossible. I was to prepare for a devastating flood by building an ark and taking along male and female pairs of every terrestrial and flying species. The task was *big!* But I felt sure I could do it by trusting God. I raced against time, but I finished it. Then the rains came. We were saved in that rockin' and reelin' ark.

106

Abraham. I am Abraham. God blessed me with many descendants. I believe God looked upon me as friend. How could I not follow God's divine instructions and go where God directed? So I left my home in Ur and set out on a sojourn following God's way. I didn't know where this journey was going to take me or what I was going to run in to. But I discovered that it is possible to continue on because of God's guidance.

Sarah. I am Sarah, the wife of Abraham. I shared Abraham's sojourn following God. Miraculously at ninety years of age, I bore our son Isaac. At first, I laughed that such a thing could happen. At that point in my life, I learned that the unexpected and miraculous is possible.

Jacob. I am Jacob, the son of Isaac and Rebekah. I became the father of Dinah and twelve sons whose names are those of the tribes of Israel. I admit that I have flaws. In fact, I have been called a trickster. But I am also known for being a settler-farmer, reverent worshiper of God, a hero, penitent brother, and benevolent father. One time, God gave me a dream of a ladder that showed the way from earth to heaven. I've learned something important about God in my life. Even with my flaws, God does not desert me. My life has always had promise with God.

Joseph. My name is Joseph, the oldest son of Rachel and son of Jacob. In my family, I became known as the spoiled son. This view of me became worse because father gave me a coat of many colors and freed me from the work required of my younger brothers. I also made the situation worse by telling them about dreams showing the important turn my life was going to take. My brothers plotted to, but did not, kill me. Instead, they did something just as bad. They sold me. In spite of this, I survived and rose from a servant in a private household to a position of administrator over grain reserves in Pharaoh's court in Egypt during a time of famine. My brothers came to buy grain for their families, but they did not recognize me. They got the grain, I finally told them who I was, and we became reconciled. All during the period of family brokenness, we had each gone on with our lives. But all the while, God was working to bring us back together.

Moses. My name is Moses. I was born to a Levite couple. At first, I was hidden. But, then, I was set adrift on a river in a water-tight container in order not to be killed in accordance with the governmental decree to kill all newborn Hebrew boys. I was picked up by Pharaoh's daughter, but I was tended by a nurse whom she hired. Although Pharaoh's daughter did not know it, the nurse was actually my natural mother. I was finally adopted by Pharaoh's daughter who gave me the name of Moses.

Even though I was reared in Pharaoh's house, I found myself identifying with the enslaved people of Israel who were my broth-ers and sisters. In fact, because I took a drastic stand in protection of one of them, I was forced to leave Egypt. I came upon a burning bush, and I was called by God to a mission to lead the enslaved people of Israel out of Egypt to the promised land. I had to persuade them that I was called to do this. God gave me the responsibility of giving them information about the journey, encouragement, chastisement when necessary, and instructions on how to get food. With God's help, we crossed the parted waters of the Red Sea out of Egypt. The people were freed from bondage.

But, even in freedom, we encountered the wilderness. Yes, we met with conflicts from outside; and there were complaints, grumblings, and rebellion from within. And, yes, there were times when I got discouraged. But then seventy others came forth to share the burden of leadership. At that point, we were all in our life struggle together leaning on God, who I know leads us and does not forsake us. I learned that our job is simply to hang in there and be faithful.

Reflection Exercise. Select one of the above first-person depictions and consider one or more ways in which the depiction reminds you of your own story plot and struggle for life meaning.

ACTIVITY 4—*Envision God's Action Today*

In activity 4, participants are invited to form groups of three. In the groups, they focus attention on the action of God in their meaning-making. They consider how their awareness of or reliance on God's acting in their lives has made possible their sense of liberating meaning and purpose. In their recall, I encourage persons to tell what happened, when it happened, how they knew God was acting, how it made them feel, and in what way(s) it brought them meaning and purpose. Where further assistance is needed, clues are drawn from how God acted in the passage from Hebrews. That is, participants are asked to recall an instance when they experienced one or more of the following:

* Awareness of receiving God's approval (Hebrews 11:2, 4).
* Being prepared by God's Word (Hebrews 11:2).
* Awareness of pleasing God (Hebrews 11:5), and being rewarded by God (Hebrews 11:8).
* Being warned by God about the future (Hebrews 11:7).
* Being called by God (Hebrews 11:8).
* Being empowered by God (Hebrews 11:11).
* Knowing that all cannot be counted on in this world, and that there is an everlasting city (Hebrews 11:16).
* Experiencing God's "raising you up" in the "dead" times of life (Hebrews 11:19).
* Recognition of abuse suffered by Christ (Hebrews 11:26).
* Remembering the many witnesses who have gone before (Hebrews 12:1).
* Reliance on Jesus the pioneer and perfecter of our faith (Hebrews 12:2).

Reflection Exercise. Using the format above, consider how God has acted in your life to bring liberating meaning and purpose.

ACTIVITY 5—*Anticipate Ongoing Response to God*

Invite participants to consider elements in their lives that threaten positive meaning-making and purpose. To assist this endeavor, I invite them to do two things. First, they write on paper one thing that needs to be changed in their individual and community life in order to bring positive meaning and purpose to them and others. Second, they write a prayer to God, asking God to direct them and their church in addressing it.

PHASE THREE: *Engaging Christian Faith Stories from the African American Heritage*

In this phase, participants link with an "African American Honor Roll of Faith." They focus on well-known and admired persons in the African American Christian faith heritage who maintained faith throughout trials and tribulations. They also discover the liberation mind-set and the liberation and vocational strategy that motivated these persons to persevere.

Activity 1—*Disclose the Faith Heritage Story*

Participants can link with the "African American Honor Roll of Faith" by participating in the following litany:

Female Leader: Sojourner Truth (1797-1883) was one of millions of enslaved people who worked to birth a nation that did not honor her humanness. She spoke of her nothingness and the insignificance of her life in the eyes of those with whom she contended for the rights due her and a whole people. In response, she became a vocal abolitionist, women's rights activist, lecturer, and religious leader. She was propelled forward in freedom's struggle, women's suffrage, and ministry with unemployed and impoverished freed people by placing her perfect trust in the soul-protecting fortress of God, the Rock. This Rock raised her above the "smallness" to which the slave system sought to reduce her. Through trust in God, she found herself raised above the battlements of fear and propelled into action.

Group: Through faith, a way was made out of no way. God was the Way-maker and Sojourner Truth followed the Way-maker.

Male Leader: Beaten and made to drink the bitterest dregs of slavery, Frederick Douglass (1818-1895) poured out his soul's complaint to the Almighty, "O, why was I born a man, of whom to make a brute! . . . I am left in the hottest hell of unending slavery. O God, save me! God, deliver me! Let me be free! Is there any God? Why am I a slave? I will run away. I will not stand it. Get caught, or get clear, I'll try it . . . I have only one life to lose. I had as well be killed running as die standing. Only think of it; one hundred miles straight north, and I'm free! Try it? Yes! God helping me, I will . . . There is a better day coming."[2] The time came when his hope overflowed, when all cowardice departed, and bold defiance took hold. Though still a slave, Frederick Douglass resolved that, though he might remain a slave in form, the day had passed when he could be a slave in fact. He called his arrival at this point "a glorious resurrection."[3] He remained firm, and on September 3, 1838, he left his chains.[4]

Group: Through faith, a way was made out of no way. God was the Way-maker and Frederick Douglass followed the Way-maker.

Female Leader: Harriet Tubman crossed the line for which she had so long dreamed. After years of cruel treatment, she was free. But she kept saying that her heart was still "down in the old cabin quarters with the old folks and my brothers and sisters."[5] Motivated by her hunger for justice, she resolved to go back to the South. She prayed to God to help her saying, "Oh, dear Lord, I ain't got no friend but you. Come to my help, Lord, for I'm in trouble!"[6] Between 1850 and 1860, she was a daring conductor on the Underground Railroad through which she guided more than three hundred slaves, including her parents, to freedom. There was a reward of twelve-thousand dollars offered for her in Maryland. It was said that she would probably be burned alive if caught. But this heroine whom the slaves called Moses was not deterred from her call to act. And, she was never caught.[7] Once a trip was started, there was no turning back. And if someone got cold feet, the voice of "Moses" rang in their ear, "Move or die!"[8] She sang to bolster the spirits of her followers, and they joined in the Spiritual "Go Down Moses": "You may hinder me here, but you can't up there, Let my people go. He sits in the heavens and answers prayer, Let my people go! Oh go down, Moses. Way down in Egypt land. Tell old Pharaoh, Let my people go!"

Group: Through faith, a way was made out of no way. God was the Way-maker, and Harriet Tubman followed the Way-maker.

Male Leader: And what more should we say? If there were time, we would tell of Dr. James W. C. Pennington, fugitive slave, teacher, clergyman, author, and civil rights activist; James

Weldon Johnson, poet and composer; Mary McLeod Bethune, educator, civil and women's rights activist, government official, and school founder; Booker T. Washington, exponent of self-improvement and racial solidarity; and W. E. B. DuBois, scholar and activist.

Female Leader: We would also tell of George Washington Carver, botanist; Zora Neal Hurston, author; Ralph Bunche, statesman and United Nations ambassador; Adam Clayton Powell, Jr., political leader and minister; Fannie Lou Hamer, civil rights activist, sharecropper; Lorraine Hansberry, playwright, activist; Jesse Owens, olympic gold medalist; Martin Luther King, Jr., minister and civil rights leader; Thurgood Marshall, lawyer and United States Supreme Court Justice; and countless more whom we name in our hearts.

Both Leaders: These are they who, through faith, continued to build up a bowed down people, followed a vision of God's promise while enduring human hostility, refused to relinquish the struggle for justice in an unjust society, and won strength out of weakness even in the face of recrimination and death.

All: Through faith, a way was made out of no way for this cloud of witnesses. God was the Way-maker, and they followed the Way-maker. Our future lies before us. Will we, like those before us, persevere, looking to Jesus the pioneer and perfecter of our faith?

ACTIVITY 2—*Describe the Liberation Mind-set*

In activity 2, three key questions are posed:

* What is the liberation mind-set that all on the "African American Honor Roll of Faith" had in common? How did this mind-set inform their life meaning and purpose?
* What are some futile mind-sets and negative life meanings and purposes the Honor Roll challenges today?

Reflection Exercise. How would you answer the questions posed above?

Actual participants have responded as follows:

"All on the honor roll had a liberation mind-set focused on freeing brothers and sisters from shackles that precluded human dignity. They wanted to assure an opportunity for brothers and sisters to participate in life unhindered by racism and the lack of life's basic necessities. This mind-set gave direction to their story plot. Meaning in their lives was derived from their own vision of liberation and their carrying out that vision."

"The Honor Roll challenges each one of us and our churches to break out of mind-sets of self-centeredness, reluctance, and fear of acting on behalf of others. These mind-sets lead to futility because when one of us is hurting, all hurt."

"Deep lasting meaning comes when we know we are helping one another. The Honor Roll convicts us to do more."

ACTIVITY 3—*Describe the Liberation Mind-Set and Liberation Vocational Strategies*

Key questions for consideration in activity 3 are:

* What generating theme made it possible for those on the "African American Honor Roll of Faith" to act on their mind-set?
* How does this theme and their acting on it challenge us today?

Reflection Exercise. How would you answer the questions posed above?

Actual participants have stated the following:

"As in the Hebrews passage, faith in God, obedience to God, and perserverance were generating themes in the lives of those on the 'African American Honor Roll of Faith.' This theme allowed them to 'keep on keeping on' in spite of difficult obstacles and hardship."

113

"Their strategy was one of really seeing the need for action and acknowledging their responsibility to act. They did not cave in and because they kept their eye on 'God, the Rock' as Sojourner Truth put it, they had a sense of power, resolve and direction."

"Both the Scripture 'Honor Roll of Faith' and the 'African American Honor Roll of Faith' give us a tremendous challenge as individuals and congregations to do likewise."

PHASE FOUR: *Engaging in Christian Ethical Decision Making*

In this final phase of the story-linking process, we focus on making decisions aimed toward positive meaning-making and life purpose based on a liberating story plot. We give particular attention to what God is calling us to do in this regard and to concrete actions we need to take.

ACTIVITY 1—*Discern God's Call*

Invite participants to call to memory as much as they can about the Scripture passage from Hebrews and the "African American Honor Roll of Faith." After the period of silent memory summation, ask each participant to choose a partner. The partners share with each other two or three points in the Scripture and the "African American Honor Roll of Faith" that particularly challenged them to look at their story plot. Partners also are asked to respond to the questions:

* What in the Scripture inspires you to act differently?
* Who would you want to emulate in the "African American Honor Roll of Faith?"

ACTIVITY 2—*Decide Concrete Actions*

Participants decide ways of responding to God's call to attend to their story plot or to change it. Participants refer to their written responses from activity 5 in phase two. At that time, they were asked to write one thing needing change in their individual and community life in order to bring positive meaning and purpose to them and others. In this activity, they respond further to this request (on paper or with a partner) according to the following:

* Identify two concrete actions you can take and two concrete actions your church can take to effect change in the matter you identified.
* Decide how far you will go to carry out the actions and how you can engage your church in action.
* Examine how the actions will contribute to your liberation and the liberation of others.
* Determine why these actions are important from a Christian viewpoint or what meanings you assign them.

The story-linking process concludes with a voluntary participant sharing and a song such as, "I Will Trust in the Lord 'Til I Die."

Follow-up Suggestions

Ask participants to form groups and list meanings African American children, teens, young adults, middle adults, and older adults assign to life. Substitute the Scripture Isaiah 40:27-31. Jeremiah 8:22 followed by Philippians 3:13b-14 may also be used. These Scriptures have particular meaning because they address the central meaning-making theme of having the spiritual resources to continue on in the midst of hardship. Because of their perseverance and spiritual resource themes, the spirituals, "Walk Together Children,"[9] and "Balm in Gilead,"[10] or the African American heritage poem "Mother to Son (Or Daughter)" by Langston Hughes[11] may be used for the heritage story.

African American sermon material may also be substituted in the heritage story phase. An example of this material is the sermon by David T. Shannon entitled "A Strange Song in a Strange Land," in *Best Black Sermons*.

The Pivotal Role of Scripture in Story-Linking and How to Choose Scripture

When knowledge comes, the whole world is turned upside down. The meaning of things begins to emerge. And more importantly, the relations between things are seen for the first time.

—*HOWARD THURMAN*
THE INWARD JOURNEY

In story-linking, the Bible is a pivotal sense-making document. It reveals the story of God through Jesus Christ by which we look at case studies, our own stories, and glean insights from African American Christian faith heritage stories. From our linking with the Bible, we are challenged to see its impact for our lives and discern how to embody its message in our lives.

We link with the Bible by bringing our everyday stories as African Americans with us. We enter the Bible with our joys. We also enter with our struggles related to experiences of oppression in this country and other everyday life struggles that block and bind us. We view and respond to the Bible through the lens of all that makes up our self-identities, social contexts, interpersonal relationships, life events, life meanings, and story plots.

The Bible has historically held special importance for the approach of African Americans to freedom from oppression and struggles. During slavery, African Americans found in the Bible a liberation pathway. Linking with the Bible became an important and dynamic way through which they heard God's call to liberation, imagined God directing and sustaining them, and decided their vocational response to God. Contemporary story-linking is a way of opening to us these same kinds of experiences with the Bible.

But what Bible stories and texts should we choose? On what basis do we choose? There are numerous stories/texts in the Bible that can place us in touch with God's speaking to us. There are also numerous accounts of biblical sojourners whose stories tell of oppressive existence, life struggles and their quest for liberation and vocation. In this chapter, we will look at three approaches to choosing Scripture for use in story-linking processes. These approaches include an historical cultural approach, a lectionary approach, and a uniform lesson materials approach. Throughout, attention will be given to the questions: How may leaders/teachers prepare for using Scripture in story-linking? What part may leaders/teachers and participants play in selecting Scripture?

An Historical Cultural Approach to Choosing Scripture

One way of determining what Bible stories/texts to use for story-linking in African American settings is to look at stories/ texts already chosen by African Americans across the years. This is best accomplished by looking at African American cultural expressions such as spirituals, hymns, gospel songs, sermons, poems, and folk sayings for references to Scripture within them.

Dating back to slavery, African Americans have had a strong biblical orientation and have relied on specific stories/texts for help in the throes of trials and tribulations. A variety of cultural expressions of African Americans shows how they linked with specific Bible stories/texts. Their choices of Scripture were cultural choices. When we select Bible stories/texts for contemporary story-linking processes from the wealth of cultural choices, we are making *historical cultural choices* of Scripture. There are at least five categories of choices:

* Old Testament freedom stories
* Old Testament and New Testament counter freedom stories
* Old Testament declaration stories
* The New Testament salvation story
* New Testament Christian life-style stories

In this chapter, we will become aware of some choices of Scripture made by African Americans from slavery onward using these categories. We will also note cultural expressions that relate to the scriptural material and that are useful in story-linking. Some of the scriptural material identified herein was incorporated in story-linking processes in chapters 2 through 4 and some were suggested for follow-up processes. Notations will be made about this use.

In preparing to use Bible stories or texts presented in this chapter, leaders/teachers will find probing the texts helpful for finding answers to the following questions:

* How does the Bible story address African American self-identity, social contexts, interpersonal relationships, life events, life meanings, and story plots?
* What answers does the Bible story give to issues arising in these facets of everyday stories?
* What hints does the story give about what liberation means and how it is attained in the various facets of life?
* What hints does the story give about what vocation means and its enactment in various facets of life?
* What relationship between liberation and vocation is disclosed in the story?

When we engage in this kind of preparatory study, we may find that certain stories/texts address a particular dimension of life, while others address more than one dimension. Suggestions for life examples are made with each Scripture indicated on the charts below.

Once a Bible story and the life dimension with which to link it are chosen, it should be incorporated into the story-linking process as illustrated in the preceding chapters. Songs, sermon material, poems, and cultural sayings may be incorporated along with Bible stories and texts or they may be used in conjunction with African American Christian faith heritage stories.

Old Testament Freedom Stories

Old Testament freedom stories are stories that disclose symbols of liberation used by African Americans. They also depict the nature of vocation through focus on leadership, relationship with God, and traits needed in the struggle to overcome oppression and adversity. Chart 1 gives examples of Old Testament freedom stories and cultural expressions reflecting them.

- -

CHART 1
OLD TESTAMENT FREEDOM STORIES

Old Testament Freedom Stories	*Cultural Expressions*
Moses' call and the freedom struggle of the Israelites, as told in Exodus 3:1-12, 13:17-22, 14:1-31	Spiritual—"Go Down, Moses"[1]
(Use in story-linking focused on interpersonal relations, life events, life meanings, and story plots)	Sermon—"The God Who Takes Off Chariot Wheels" by D. E. King[2]
Daniel in the Lion's Den, as told in chapter 6 of the book of Daniel	Spiritual—"Didn't My Lord Deliver Daniel?"[3]
(Use with self-identity, social contexts, interpersonal relations and life events)	
David and Goliath, as told in 1 Samuel 17:1-51.	Spiritual—"Little David, Play on Your Harp"[4]

(Use with interpersonal relations, life events, life meanings and story plots)	Sermon—"Giants Keep Coming" by William Watley[5]

The three Hebrew boys (Shadrach, Meshach, and Abednego) in the fiery furnace, as told in Daniel 3:1-30	Incorporated in the prior cited spiritual—"Didn't My Lord Deliver Daniel?"
(Use with self-identity, social contexts, interpersonal relations and life events)	

Jonah in and out of the belly of the whale, as found in the four short chapters 1 through 4 in the book of Jonah	Incorporated in the prior cited spiritual—"Didn't My Lord Deliver Daniel?"
(Use with every facet of the everyday stories	

Old Testament and New Testament Counter Freedom Stories

African American Christians across the years have also chosen counter freedom stories in Scripture. The gists of these stories appear in African American preaching material and oral folk sayings. The stories are characterized by bondage and subservience themes by which persons in the larger social structure have justified oppression. Meanings are assigned to these stories / texts in light of counter liberation themes marking the everyday stories of African Americans. These meanings invariably depict an understanding of the positive value God places on us over against devaluation by other humans. In short, the counter freedom stories are typical of biblical texts with which we have historically critically engaged from inside our experiences. In the engagement process, we deviate from literal interpretations, thereby giving new light to texts that contradict our understanding of God's value and liberating activity through Jesus for *all*. The following are examples of counter freedom stories:

* "Curse of Ham" found in Genesis 9:20-27.
* Paul's encouragement of slaves to be obedient to their masters, found in Ephesians 6:5 and Colossians 3:22.
* Paul's sending the slave Onesimus back to his master, detailed in the book of Philemon.

One example of an African American folk saying focuses on reinterpreting the counter liberation story of Hagar and Ishmael, found in Genesis 16:1-6 and 21:8-21. The folk saying was handed down through my maternal grandmother and was one shared by other African Americans in the Indiana town of my birth. In the folk saying, Hagar was given the affectionate name of "Aunt Haggie" and Ishmael was referred to as "Aunt Haggie's child." Entitled "Aunt Haggie," the folk saying is as follows:

> People may treat you like they did "Aunt Haggie" or like one of "Aunt Haggie's children," but you don't have to act like you're not important or be ashamed of who you are. It doesn't matter who you are, you hear? You just remember, you're one of God's children.

Like the liberation stories in the Bible, the counter freedom stories may be chosen for use in contemporary story-linking processes. They are an important way of opening to persons a way of talking about dehumanizing and hurtful attitudes and treatment and what the overall message of the Bible is for their response to these attitudes and treatment. Recall that both the text from Genesis and the African American folk saying are suggested as follow-up material at the end of chapter 2 which focuses on self-identity and social contexts.

Old Testament Declaration Stories

Historical cultural choices of biblical material also include texts that declare feelings, attitudes, desires, and behaviors often associated with the struggle for liberation and vocation. Some of the texts declare often inexplicable agony and hurt amidst trial and tribulation. This type of declaration story has a theme of theodicy, which means suffering and anguish. Other declaration stories reveal the possibility and, indeed, the presence of guidance, assurance, thanksgiving, and jubilation in life's sojourn. This second type of declaration story exemplifies themes of promise and celebration. Texts from the Psalms and Jeremiah have been among the most popular choices of declaration stories. African American choices of texts with theodicy themes show that faith does not always cancel disappointment, oppression, and bondage and that we do not always see concretely God's liberating work. In story-linking, these stories offer an avenue for persons to give voice openly to their laments to God at times when their faith in God's righteousness is not easy and they are in search of wisdom. Examples of declaration stories with theodicy themes and related cultural expressions appear in chart 2.

- -

CHART 2
OLD TESTAMENT DECLARATION STORIES
WITH THEODICY THEMES

Old Testament Declaration Stories with Theodicy Themes	*Cultural Expressions*
Psalm 22:1-11	Spiritual—"Don't leave me, Lord, Don't leave me behin'."
(Use with all facets of the everyday stories)	
Psalm 13	Slave narratives—"Oh, Lord, how long? Oh, Lord, how long?"[6] and, "Oh, Lord Jesus, how long, how long shall I suffer this way?"[7]
(Use with all facets of the everyday stories)	

Jeremiah 8:22

(Use with all facets of the every-day stories)

The slaves answered the question with the spiritual "There is a balm in Gilead to make the wounded whole. There is a balm in Gilead to heal the sinsick soul. Sometimes I feel discouraged and think my work's in vain. But then the Holy Spirit revives my soul again."[8]

Recall that Psalm 13 is suggested for follow-up at the end of chapter 3 which focuses on interpersonal relationships and life events. In chapter 4 on life meanings and story plots, Jeremiah 8:22 is suggested as a follow-up companion text with a New Testament text along with the spiritual, "Balm in Gilead" and sermon material. However, any of the texts mentioned above may be considered for follow-up in chapters 2 through 4.

African Americans choose texts from which promise and celebration are found. Of particular significance are texts in the book of Psalms and in Isaiah. These texts have historically provided a "bowed-down" people resources to "keep on keeping on" in the midst of trial and tribulation. In story-linking, the texts appropriately function as companions to counter freedom stories and declaration stories with theodicy themes. They should be used as companion texts because they offer responses to persons' search for wisdom when considering counter freedom stories and declaration stories with theodicy themes.

African American choices of "declaration stories" that have promise and celebration themes are reflected particularly in spirituals, gospel songs, and sermon material. For this reason, singing spirituals and gospel songs and looking at sermon materials are important additions to the process of linking with these Scriptures. Chart 3 below contains examples of texts that may be considered declaration stories with themes of promise or celebration. Cultural expressions reflecting the themes accompany the Bible texts as does one sermon title.

CHART 3
OLD TESTAMENT DECLARATION STORIES WITH THEMES OF PROMISE OR CELEBRATION

Old Testament Declaration Stories with Themes of Promise or Celebration	*Cultural Expressions*
Psalm 23 (Use with all facets of the everyday stories)	We shall walk through the valley and the shadow of death; We shall walk through the valley in peace. If Jesus Himself shall be our leader, we shall walk through the valley in peace.
Psalm 27 (Use with all facets of the everyday stories)	"I will trust in the Lord. I will trust in the Lord 'til I die."[9] Also, the gospel song: "The Lord is my light and my salvation . . . Whom shall I fear? . . . The Lord is the strength of my life. Of whom shall I be afraid?"
Psalms 33 and 104 (See suggestion for Psalm 33:13-22 as follow-up at end of chapter 3)	"He's got the whole world in His hands. He's got the birds and the bees right in His hands. He's got the itty bitty baby in His hands. He's got you and me, sister, in His hands. He's got you and me brother, in His hands."[10]
Isaiah 40:27-31 (See suggestion for use of text and song at end of chapter 4)	"Walk together, children, don't you get weary. Walk together, children, don't you get weary. Oh, talk together, children, don't you get weary, there's a great camp meeting in the Promised land."[11]

Also, William Watley's sermon entitled "God Calls Us to Be Eagles"[12]

The New Testament Salvation Story

For African Americans, the New Testament salvation story emphasizes the person of Jesus. This includes Jesus' parables, sayings, acts, and character that herald him as the great champion of freedom. Underlying the salvation story is the historical understanding among African Americans that Jesus as champion of freedom shows us how to live liberating and vocation-centered stories. Options of Bible texts that show this understanding along with cultural expressions reflecting it are contained in charts 4A, 4B, and 4C below.

CHART 4A
THE NEW TESTAMENT SALVATION STORY:
PARABLES OF JESUS

Parables and Sayings of Jesus	*Cultural Expressions*
Matthew 7:24-27 or Luke 6:47-49	"I got a home in-a dat Rock, don't don't you see."[13]
(Use with every facet of the everyday story)	
Matthew 5:14-16 (See suggestion for use in chapter 2)	"This little light of mine, I'm goin' to let it shine."[14]
Matthew 22:1-14 or Luke 14:15-24 Use with story-linking focused on self-identity and social context)	"I'm goin' to eat at the welcome table, O yes, I'm goin' to eat at the welcome table some of these days hallelujah!"[15]

125

CHART 4B
THE NEW TESTAMENT SALVATION STORY:
ACTS OF JESUS

Acts of Jesus	*Gospel Songs and Spirituals*
Mark 4:35-41, Matthew 9:2-8, or Luke 5:17-26	"The Old Ship of Zion," (see esp. verse 2)[16]
(Use with story-linking focused on self-identity and social con- texts, interpersonal relations, and life events)	

Mark 2:1-12, Matthew 9:2-8, or Luke 8:22-25	"O Lamb, Beautiful Lamb"[17]
(See suggestion for use in chapter 3)	

CHART 4C
THE NEW TESTAMENT SALVATION STORY:
THE CHARACTER OF JESUS

Character of Jesus	*Gospel Songs and Spirituals*
John 1:1-5, *Jesus as Light*	"Walk in the Light, Beautiful Light"[18]
(Use with all facets of everyday stories)	

Luke 12:4-7 and Matthew 10:26-31, *Jesus as Friend*	"His Eye Is on the Sparrow"[19]
(Use with all facets of everyday stories)	

Matthew 25:1-13.
Jesus as Challenger to Tend to the
work of Liberating vocation

"Members, Don't Get Weary"[20]

Use with all facets of everyday
stories)

- -

Luke 18:35-43,
Matthew 20:29-34 or
Mark 10:46-52. See also: Luke
17:11-16 and Mark 2:1-12, *Jesus as*
Powerful, Caring and Merciful.

"De Blin' Man Stood on de Road
an' Cried"[21]

(See suggested use of Mark 2:1-
12 in chapter 3.)

- -

Luke 2:8-20. Also, Mark 15:16-39,
Matt. 27:27-56, Luke 23:26-49, or
John 19:16*b*-30,
Jesus as Vulnerable, Humble,
Sacrificial.

(Use with every facet of the
everyday story)

"Sweet little Jesus Boy, they
made you be born in a manger.
Sweet little Holy Chile, they
didn't know who you wuz. The
world treat you mean, Lord.
Treat me mean too. But dat's
how things is down here. They
didn't know t'was you."[22]
Also:
"Were You There when They Cru-
cified My Lord?"[23]

- -

Mark 14:22-26, Matthew 26:26-29,
or Luke 22:14-23, *Jesus as Com-*
memorator of God's Liberating
Love

(Use with every facet of the
everyday story)

"Let Us Break Bread Together"[24]

- -

Luke 23:26-34,
Jesus as Forgiving Saviour

(Use with every facet of the
everyday story

"Remember Me"[25]

- -

New Testament Christian Life-style Stories

Historically, African Americans have chosen New Testament texts that describe the nature of the Christian life one is expected to live regardless of one's situation. The spirituals in particular show that Christian life is lived after the example of Jesus Christ, the champion of freedom. They show God's plan for liberation and vocation is carried forward through committed Christian living by *all* who accept God's call. That includes us! Biblical texts and cultural expressions appear in chart 5 below.

CHART 5
NEW TESTAMENT CHRISTIAN
LIFE-STYLE STORIES

Christian Life-style	*Cultural Expressions*
Ephesians 4:11-16 *Live in Christ's Fullness* (Use with every facet of the everyday stories)	The theme of the biblical text is found in a poem by former slave, Walter L. Brooks entitled "The Stature of the Fullness of Christ."[26] Also: "Lord, I Want to Be a Christian"[27]
Galatians 6:1-10 *Live By the Spirit of Jesus in Community* (Use with every facet of the everyday story	"Walk Together, Children"[28]
Hebrews 10:39, 11:1-39, 12:1-2 *Live by Faith, Commitment, Perserverance* (See suggestion for use of text in chapter 4).	"Who'll Be a Witness"[29] Also: "Done made my vow to the Lord, and I never will turn back. I will go, I shall go to see what the end will be."[30]

Prospects and Problems of Using the Historical Cultural Approach to Choosing Scripture

The historical cultural approach to choosing Bible texts is a pivotal prospect for story-linking processes. It is pivotal because it takes full account of the African American cultural context. It helps leaders/teachers and participants to correlate Scripture with the biblically oriented and culturally rich African American tradition. The approach holds potential for heightening our awareness of how African Americans, past and present, have linked with Scripture. It promotes claiming our cultural and biblical roots as African Americans.

The historical cultural approach also opens the way for leaders/teachers *and* participants to draw on revered Bible stories and texts, biblically based songs, cultural sayings, and sermon material related to the Bible. In this way, choosing Bible stories is not the sole responsibility of leaders/teachers. Instead, leaders/teachers encourage participants to contribute through materials they bring. Participants bring into the story-linking processes the biblical and cultural resources that are important to them, and they share why these resources are important. Moreover, when participants take part in story-linking in this way, the process becomes their process.

The historical cultural approach is most easily employed in Christian education settings where leaders/teachers and participants are knowledgeable of biblical and cultural resources. That is, the approach is best carried forth when persons have had prior experiences with Bible storytelling and story-listening, African American faith heritage songs, cultural sayings, and sermons. Problems of accessing, choosing, and using appropriately these resources may arise in settings where leaders/teachers or participants have had limited exposure and involvement with them. Nonetheless, the problems can be overcome through two steps initiated by leaders/teachers.

The first step is to seek biblical and cultural materials in libraries and bookstores and carefully review the materials. Commentaries and reference works on these materials are also helpful. The purpose for reviewing the materials is to determine how biblical mate-

rials and cultural resources such as heritage songs, cultural sayings, and sermon material relate to one another. This means seeking to answer the questions, What Bible stories or texts are
reflected in these cultural resources? How are the stories told in the
cultural resources? Why?

The second step is to identify facets of the everyday African
American stories with which the Bible texts and cultural materials may be linked. The way to do this is through seeing
similarities between issues addressed in Bible texts and cultural materials and those addressed in the everyday stories. It
is helpful to link the biblical and cultural materials with all
facets of everyday African American stories to which they give
guidance. Repetitive use of both biblical and cultural materials
reminds leaders/teachers and participants that Scripture speaks
to us in many different ways. Repetition also contributes to our
remembering these materials and claiming them as vital instruc-
tional agents in our quests for liberation and vocation.

The Lectionary Approach to Choosing Scripture

Particularly in settings where experiences with biblical and
cultural resources are limited, consulting the lectionary offers
another approach to choosing Scripture for story-linking processes. The lectionary is a list of selected Bible texts for each
Sunday of the church year. The Bible texts entered for each
Sunday include a Psalm, a text from the Old Testament, one from
the New Testament Epistles, and one from the New Testament
Gospels. These selections form what is called Revised Common
Lectionary. The lectionary is generally established for a three-
year period, or according to a triennial calendar labeled as years
A, B, and C. The calendars are often found in church hymnbooks,
other church worship materials, and in *The Lectionary Bible*.[31]
They provide a guide that shows which texts are to be used on a
given Sunday.

In using the Revised Common Lectionary in story-linking,
we actually link facets of everyday African American stories
with biblical stories that correspond with the various seasons
of the Christian year. That is, biblical material focused around

the seasons of Advent, Christmas, Epiphany, Lent, Easter, Pentecost, and other special days provide the overall framework for story-linking processes. We still pose the question, What does the Scripture have to say for liberation and vocation in terms of our identity, social contexts, interpersonal relations, life events, and story plots? However, the lectionary approach invites the added question, How do the various seasons of the Christian year and the church's observance of them contribute to our liberation and vocation in these facets of our lives?

Prospects and Problems of Using the Lectionary Approach to Choosing Scripture for Story-Linking

A primary contribution of the lectionary approach to story-linking processes is its provision of predetermined Bible texts. Since they are already provided in the lectionary, leaders/teachers do not have to decide on Bible texts. The lectionary approach also challenges us to incorporate Bible stories that are new to us and that offer us new ways of seeing our everyday stories. And the lectionary invites us to consider whether and how our African American believing communities interpret our everyday lives and our liberation and vocation in light of the Christian year.

A key problem in using the lectionary approach is the dominance of the Christian calendar. Because of this dominance, it may not be possible to incorporate in fullest measure historic culturally revered Bible texts and other cultural materials. Nonetheless, it is possible for leaders/teachers to employ a planning method that can maximize the use of important contextual materials in story-linking processes. This method builds on one proposed by Dieter T. Hessel and incorporates the following:

1. Experience and question the Bible story with focus on finding out what is going on in the text. Take note of the setting, story movement, and story actors.
2. Explore whether and how the story addresses identity, social contexts, interpersonal relationships, life events, life meanings, and story plot. Take note of evidences of liberating activity and vocation.

3. Explore in commentaries the role of the story in its biblical setting.
4. Discover what God is doing in the story.
5. Discern what the text says for decisions you may make that can bring about greater and ongoing experiences of liberation and vocation.
6. Reflect critically on the church's faithful response to the Bible story in its life of worship, education, and nurture during the Christian season being emphasized.
7. Discern what changes are needed in the life of the church to promote liberation and vocation in the various facets of everyday life.[32]

The Uniform Lesson Series Approach to Choosing Scripture for Story-Linking

A third approach to choosing Scripture for story-linking processes entails use of Scripture contained in uniform lesson series. Like the lectionary approach, the uniform lesson series approach does not require leaders/teachers to select Bible texts. The texts are preselected in a way that is designed to cover the entire Bible in a six-year cycle. Over the cycle, nearly every book of the Bible is dealt with in some fashion within church school and Bible study materials for the various age levels.[33]

Prospects and Problems of Using the Uniform Lesson Approach to Choosing Scripture for Story-Linking

The uniform lesson approach provides a helpful alternative approach to choosing Scripture for story-linking processes because many local churches use the uniform lesson series in church school. This means that the series is already available to leaders/teachers and participants. Since the series is designed to cover the whole Bible over a six-year cycle, and incorporates planned lessons, historic culturally revered Bible stories will be included. Moreover, the series invites linking with unfamiliar texts.

The problem is that texts that have particular contextual meaning may not appear when they are desired or when they may have greatest impact. Nonetheless, the approach does not preclude leaders/teachers use of the seven-step planning approach described above in order to assure applicability to the precise concerns of story-linking.

Reflection Exercise. Consider the three approaches to choosing Scripture for story-linking processes. Take some time to plan a story-linking experience based on each one of the approaches. After you choose the Scripture, be sure to experience the Scripture and determine which life dimensions it addresses. Then, consider how you will present it in phase two of the story-linking process as outlined at the end of chapter 1. You may wish to refer again to the illustrations of the story-linking process in chapters 2 through 4.

CHAPTER 6 _____

Mediating Group Processes

Our shoulders touch but our hearts cry out for understanding with-out which there can be no life and no meaning. . . . There must be found ever-creative ways that can ventilate the private soul without blowing it away, that can confirm and affirm the integrity of the person.

HOWARD THURMAN
THE INWARD JOURNEY

I n guiding groups through the story-linking process, I have found that groups and individuals within them differ in how they engage the process and interact with one another. Some whole groups "dive in" with exuberant participation. Others are less talkative in the beginning and gradually "grow into" open and depthful participation. Some individuals are readily self-disclosive while others are not; and some prefer quiet reflection to more expressive forms. Some individuals also enjoy and have capacities for facilitating small groups while others prefer the participant role.

The groups reminded me of the importance of paying attention to group processes and dynamics in implementing the story-linking model. Indeed, I believe attentiveness to group processes and dynamics is essential if we are to create an environment that embodies the essence of liberation and vocation toward which story-linking points. But what is meant by group processes and group dynamics, and how do we take them into account as leaders/teachers in the story-linking process?

Group processes refer to the strategies or plan of action leaders/teachers take to ensure an emancipatory environment. The term *group dynamics* refers to the forces and conditions that influence how group members participate and relate with one another in the story-linking process. We cannot separate the two because each impacts the other. This chapter presents five elements that I have found helpful in attending to group processes and dynamics. These elements include approaches to convening groups, knowing developmental stages of groups, tending to group membership and size, time management, and constructing inviting physical settings.

Approaches to Convening Groups

How we get started in the story-linking process is important. It can make a difference in persons' decisions to enter and fully engage in the process in a group setting and elsewhere. One pivotal approach to convening groups entails the leader's welcoming presence. Another key approach involves sharing the nature of the story-linking process into which persons are being invited. A final approach is to invite interpersonal connection.

The Welcoming Presence of Leaders/Teachers

The role of the leader or teacher includes offering a welcoming presence. This means that we value and appreciate those who join us in the story-linking process as they are, and we express openly our appreciation for their presence with us and for the opportunity to relate together. The welcoming presence of the leader/teacher reflects the Christian understanding of *agape love* mentioned in the prologue. Stated another way, the practice of *agape love* through a welcoming presence becomes an important promoter of liberating and vocation-centered action within the group.

Our role as a welcoming presence based on *agape love* also means that we are not hesitant to say and to show through our nonverbal expression that we are glad to be together. Expressions of positive value and appreciation of persons is particularly important in African American Christian education settings because of the negative valuing we often receive in everyday social contexts.

Positive valuing and expressions of appreciation given by leaders is a way of affirming our being in solidarity. It is also a way of saying to persons that their presence is not being taken for granted. This kind of welcoming presence encourages openness in communication among participants and builds within them a sense of security. With this presence, we recognize that persons are most guarded when they feel unsure how they will be received.

Sharing the Nature of the Story-Linking Process

Because story-linking is a particular approach to Christian education, it is helpful to let participants know the nature of the process. This gives participants a glimpse of where we are headed in the process as well as offering them tools with which to engage in story-linking on their own. It is important for leaders/teachers to share with participants that they are invited into a four-phase story-linking process. This means that they will look at everyday African American stories. They will link these stories with the Christian faith story contained in the Bible. They will also link with African American Christian faith heritage stories. And they will learn to practice Christian decision making. Actually, it is wise to re-identify the four story-linking phases at the beginning of each session.

Participants need to know, as well, that story-linking focuses on liberation and vocation in the various facets of our everyday stories. For this reason, it is important that we share with groups that we will invite them into dialogue about what liberation and vocation mean.

As stated earlier, story-linking is appropriately undertaken in settings where intentional efforts are made to create an environment where *agape love* is practiced. In such an environment, we give people voice and we commit to hear and to respond to them with care, support, and attentive listening. How do we begin to create this environment?

Inviting Persons into Interpersonal Connection

I like to begin each story-linking session with a short period (not exceeding ten minutes) during which group members engage in what I call "Making Interpersonal Connections." Thus, the first phase of the story-linking process begins only after the group has "connected." Making interpersonal connections can be whole-group oriented or they may be partner or small group oriented.

Making Interpersonal Connections in Whole Group Settings

Making interpersonal connections in groups encompasses the need for participants to disclose something about themselves before the whole group. The disclosures may begin with "connection starters" given by the leader/teacher, of which the following are examples:

* Invite group members to complete starters like:
  "I am . . . "
  "One thing you may not know about me is . . . "
  "The person I admire most is . . . " and "I admire that person because. . . "
  "The best thing about my life is . . . "
  "The most challenging thing about my life is . . . "
* Invite group members to tell about an occurrence in the previous week or recent past that gave them joy, assurance, or hope.
* Invite group members to share a concern for which they desire group prayer.
* Invite group members to tell the name and words of their favorite religious song or Bible verse and why they are favorites. This may be followed by singing songs of which all group members are familiar.

Making interpersonal connections in the whole group helps us learn about one another, even if we are related or have been previously acquainted. It also builds group openness, fosters responsiveness toward one another, and promotes group solidarity.

After each member's disclosure, group members may be invited to respond by saying, "Thank you for sharing."

Making Interpersonal Connections in Small Groups

Participants may also make interpersonal connections with a partner or in a small group of no more than four persons. In this instance, leaders/teachers guide persons to share something about themselves with a partner or small group members. The connection starters above may be used for this purpose. It is preferable to form different partners and different small group membership if you use that format repeatedly.

Partner and small group connections emphasize caring, attentive listening and developing the ability to reflect back what another has shared. Thus partners and small group members are invited to practice repeating what they hear others say and receiving clarification from others when needed. It is also helpful to invite partners and small group members to determine ways of giving caring, affirming, and supportive responses to one another. Persons might respond to one another, for example, by saying: "I appreciate what you shared," or "Thank you for sharing." They might also agree to say prayers of thanks or prayers of intercession for one another.

Reflection Exercise. Develop a specific strategy that you might use to convene a group in which you intend to use the story-linking process.

Knowing Developmental Stages of Groups

How leaders/teachers mediate group processes depends on a complex set of factors. Some of the key factors include how long a group has been together, whether the leader/teacher is new to her or his role with a group, what kind of interpersonal style has been developed in groups of long-standing, and what kind of interpersonal style the leader/teacher fosters.

It is also good to recognize that groups typically develop in stages. Newly constituted groups with whom leaders/teachers have had no prior contact typically go through an initial stage of orientation or encounter. New groups may then move to a stage characterized by conflict, dominance, and differentiation. During a third stage, group members may move to a sense of group cohesiveness, and group productivity. Finally, a group may move to a stage characterized by free and constructive movement between independence and interdependence. Awareness of these stages provides bases for deciding what is needed to mediate group processes and respond to group dynamics. Two examples of groups with which I have been associated are illustrative of the presence of group stages:

Case Example 1

One group with whom I introduced the story-linking process was an intergenerational church school class. They had been meeting prior to my joining them and had developed an attentive but passive style of participation. In the beginning, it was clear that they took a somewhat wait-and-see stance. At times, a group member would firmly suggest that we might want to go in another direction from the one toward which we had begun. However, as we continued our weekly sessions, the group members became more and more centered on connecting their situations with the stories in the story-linking process. The group members became increasingly active in the process. Self-disclosures in both the whole group and in small groups gradually came forth freely from nearly every group member. Group members encouraged and supported one another in their sharing and in their choice to be silent. Each person felt free to get their points across. Getting to this point did not happen quickly. It happened over time. The number of group members also grew.

Case Example 2

I had been the leader of one group over a short period of time. When we entered into the story-linking process, the group had already moved through a testing period where some group members tended to dominate group discussion. With the beginning of story-linking, they quickly established a mutuality-oriented rapport. In the beginning, small group members readily pressed capable leaders into service. But, over time, leadership began to rotate. Those who tended to be quiet blossomed in small groups. This gave them courage to share in the whole group setting. There were, in fact, some surprises as persons thought to be very quiet shared their stories in great detail. The group's functioning became that of support group. In some instances, one might say that they got carried away with the process and did not want to stop at certain points in the process. They hoped that the group would always continue as it is.

We will explore the dynamics encountered in the developmental stages of groups and how these dynamics are represented in the case examples. We will also explore ways of mediating group processes in light of the stages.

Group Processes During Orientation or Encounter

During the stage of orientation or encounter, group members are uncertain and can be reluctant to share openly. They are concerned about inclusion, acceptance, and solidarity. They also desire clear leadership that is nonthreatening. In Case Example 1, this stage was represented in the group's wait-and-see stance. The first stage was not demonstrably present in Case Example 2 because it had occurred prior to their entry into the story-linking process. Groups at this stage can benefit greatly from the kinds of approaches to convening groups presented earlier. But it is important for leaders/teachers not to compel persons to share. Group members must be allowed freedom to build a personal sense of comfortability with personal story disclosure within the group setting. If group members respond with reluctance or silence to leader/teacher invitations to whole group sharing, the leader/teacher may move to partner or small group sharing. Sharing in this way can be far less threatening than sharing in a whole group.

Leaders/teachers may also note group members who have difficulty speaking spontaneously. In situations where this kind of difficulty arises, the use of partners or small groups is also warranted. Moreover, if partners or small groups are asked to report back to the whole group, they may be invited before they report to record what they will say on paper or newsprint.

Group Processes During Conflict, Dominance, and Differentiation

Groups move with varying degrees of rapidity into a stage characterized by conflict, dominance, and differentiation. Evidence of a group's movement into this stage can be noted by struggles of group members to reach consensus, dominance of some group members over others, and increased desire among group members to identify the direction the group should go. In Case Example 1, a group member firmly suggested that we might want to go in another direction. In Case 2, the group tested the leadership prior to entering into the story-linking process.

Leaders/teachers who recognize the second stage as a normal development of group dynamics are better able to mediate group processes. As groups move into this stage, it is helpful to use the technique of brainstorming. In story-linking, this technique is helpful where group reflection on everyday stories, Bible texts, the faith heritage stories, and Christian decision making are requested. Whether in whole groups or small groups, brainstorming entails first the gathering of ideas without comment. Group discussion and evaluative statements follow.

A second technique in this stage is to pose scenarios such as "If you were to respond to the meaning of this everyday story (or Bible text, or heritage story), what would you say?" Or, "If you were to decide to take personal or group action in response to the story-linking we have done, what would you do?" This technique gives opportunity for individual responses to emerge and to be pooled together. Whole groups, partners, or small groups can then be invited to enter into discussion on how to go about prioritizing the responses.

An additional technique that is useful in this stage is role playing. When there are repeated opportunities to role play, group members are afforded opportunities to exchange what may be perceived as leading and supportive roles. This is also a way of allowing leadership to emerge from within the group in a rather controlled fashion.

The role of leaders/teachers is not a passive one. Indeed, it is important that leaders/teachers take on a process-observer role in which they observe carefully the behavior of group members and help to facilitate the process of working sensitively together.

Group Processes During Group Cohesiveness and Productivity

The stage of cohesiveness and group productivity is characterized by mutual functioning. Persons are at ease in self-disclosing, and they move through story-linking in a free and relaxed manner. Persons are comfortable with both the group and the story-linking process. In Case Example 1, the group members became increasingly active in the process, free in their self-disclosure and encouraging and supportive of one another. In Case Example 2, the group members quickly established a mutuality-oriented process.

In this stage, the mutual sojourner role of the leader/teacher and group members can be fully exercised. Even though participants look to the leader/teacher as the one ultimately responsible for group processes, they are able to see the leader/teacher as partner in the story-linking process. This assumes, however, that the leader/teacher has been and continues to be a welcoming presence and an active, sensitive, and disclosive participant throughout the process.

Group Processes During Constructive Independence and Interdependence

In the stage characterized by constructive independence and interdependence, the participants are fully invested in their own and others' discerning what the story-linking process has to say to them. They develop a group consciousness and a consciousness of their belonging in the group. Persons express their interest in the group's continuing to meet and in their own continued engagement in the story-linking process. In Case Example 1, this stage was evidenced in working group relationships that allowed each person to get their points across. In Case Example 2, individuals shared within a support group atmosphere, and they did not want the group to end.

This last developmental stage of group process is both a rewarding and a challenging one. It is rewarding because of the excitement and meaning that is generated in groups at this stage. But a challenge can emerge when groups exhibit ingrown and exclusive tendencies. These tendencies become evident when groups show contentment only with what takes place in the group. They may show inhospitable attitudes toward new group members. There may be limited follow-through on decisions for action made by group members in phase four of the story-linking process. Group members may also seek to lengthen previously agreed upon meeting times beyond what is actually feasible or comfortable. When groups exhibit these tendencies, they move away from liberating and vocation-focused dynamics. The role of the leader/teacher is to identify any tendencies toward ingrown group dynamics and to re-orient the group again toward more liberating and vocation-centered ends.

Leaders/teachers may approach this situation by naming what is taking place without placing blame on others and by giving direct guidance. We may say, for example, "I feel uneasy about the direction in which we seem to be going. I would like for us to direct our attention to a time line for carrying out the decisions we make in our story-linking today and commit to a report on them at the end of the time line." Similarly, we may guide groups to look at how they may develop welcoming strategies for newcomers and may address the length of story-linking sessions. Additional attention will be given to group membership and size as well as time management in the following sections.

Reflection Exercise. Review the stages of group process. Recall any experiences you have had of proceeding through these stages either as a group participant or a group leader.

Tending to Group Membership and Size

It is important to give some attention to group membership and size because each exerts some influence on group processes and dynamics. We will give particular attention to the impact of intergenerational group membership on group dynamics and processes in story-linking. We will also explore ways of mediating intergenerational groups.

Group Membership

Story-linking is a process for intergenerational participation in church, community, home, and retreat settings. Intergenerational participation refers to the communal engagement in story-linking through face-to-face sharing of persons from two or more generations or life stages. (Older adults, middle-aged adults, young adults, youths, and children)

Through intergenerational group membership, we seek to create communal-oriented group dynamics. We promote these dynamics when we foster appreciation for one another's uniqueness. We also promote these dynamics when we acknowledge the contribution each person from the various generations can make to story-linking and one another's liberation and vocation. However, accomplishing this requires that we understand generational differences, conflict, and difficulties in intergenerational group interaction.

Generational Differences

African Americans bring to story-linking the experiences and behaviors associated with their particular life stages. African Americans from each life stage also bring personal values and views informed by the specific era in which they were born and reared. These stage-specific factors produce generational differences.

Generational differences can cause conflict or create resistance when persons criticize, confront, blame, or reject one another. This kind of conflict can either discourage intergenerational participation or create a restrictive atmosphere. Moreover, group members may not understand the benefit of positive or creative conflict in which persons encourage one another to share their perspectives and strive to hear and respond in respectful ways to different perspectives.

Persons may also have difficulty entering into intergenerational participation in story-linking because they are unaccustomed to this kind of participation in Christian education. For some, this kind of difficulty may derive from customary participation in stage-based or age-based Christian education experiences. The question is, "How do we mediate group processes given these several types of dynamics?"

Mediating Intergenerational Group Processes

Prior to entering into story-linking with an intergenerational group, it is important that leaders confirm within themselves the value of such a group. Leaders must feel secure in their own life stage and uniqueness and their ability to affirm the value and uniqueness of others. They should ask themselves these questions:

* Do you affirm the right and the need of African Americans from the various life stages to share their perspectives?
* Are you willing to invest deeply in a loving and caring group process?
* Do you recognize your own limitations and biases?
* Are you willing to continually tend to the sensitivities of others?

How leaders/teachers function in the actual intergenerational group setting is pivotal to how persons from differing generations relate to one another. When we function as mutual sojourners in the story-linking process and are relaxed and open, we encourage the same functioning in group members. We show ourselves as mutual sojourners in the intergenerational setting when we self-disclose willingly, freely express affirming caring feelings, maintain eye contact with others who are talking, and listen attentively so that others can accept responsibility for speaking.

Leaders/teachers are also responsible for involving the intergenerational group in the actual story-linking process in positive ways. I have found three approaches helpful.

First, create nonthreatening opportunities for persons to share their thoughts, ideas, and insights. This may be promoted by asking indirect questions, particularly in the beginning of the story-linking process. To do this, we invite persons to "talk through" the actors in case studies, Bible stories/texts, and African American faith heritage stories. For example, we may ask: Who in the stories are of greatest interest to you and why? Who were of least interest and why? In what ways do you think the stories tell about things that happen today? As persons become more comfortable in responding to indirect questions, we may move to more direct questions such as: In what ways do you see yourself in the stories? How do the stories speak to you in your situation?

Second, persons of every life stage tend to respond actively to role playing, dramatizations, and singing and can, therefore, be readily integrated into these activities. It is especially helpful to use role playing or dramatizations where everyone has a part or that are easily repeated so that parts may be rotated.

In using songs, however, it is important to be sensitive to the differing musical tastes of persons in the various stages. It is helpful to give a forthright invitation to group members to choose, sing, and even teach one another to sing their favorite spirituals, gospel songs, or hymns. Such an invitation communicates the leader's/teacher's understanding of the enrichment derived from intergenerational sharing of music.

Third, we may promote positive intergenerational participation by using small groups during response and reflection periods in the story-linking process. Leaders/teachers should not hesitate to invite small groups to consider how they can encourage the active participation of all members. To do this, leaders/teachers set as expectations the group members' attentive and respectful response to one another. We may ask small group members to seek a consensus on ground rules regarding rotation of group leaders, recorders, and spokespersons for the group.

Where children are present, small group members may integrate them into the group by retelling stories used in story-linking in shortened, condensed form and in ways that emphasize the role of children in the stories. They may then ask a child to tell the stories in the child's own words. The small group then undertakes a discussion about the meaning of the stories and includes the children in the discussion.

Reflection Exercise. Envision how you would mediate in positive ways an intergenerational group comprised of adults, youths, and children.

Group Size

The size of a group will have some bearing on group processes and dynamics. The story-linking process is suitable for as few as two persons. In this case, there is no leader/teacher. The two persons merely engage in a mutual dialogue and reflection following the phases of the story-linking process. When various sizes of family groupings, church school groups, or retreat groups engage in story-linking, the designated leader mediates the group process according to the information provided above. Generally, active group participation can be attained more easily in small groups of up to ten persons. In groups that exceed ten persons, it is helpful to utilize partners and small groups of three or four persons who can provide a sense of closeness and intimacy in dialogue and reflection.

Reflection Exercise. Envision how you would engage in the story-linking process with one other person who is younger or older than yourself. Then envision how you would lead either a small group of four to five family members or another group of ten or more persons in story-linking.

Time Management

Each story-linking session is designed to take about one and one-half hours. If time does not permit completion of the process in a single session and several days will elapse before your next time together, the process is best undertaken in segments. When it is segmented, phases one and two may be completed in one session. Phases three and four may be completed in a successive session. Dividing story-linking in this way allows for more cohesive movement through the process.

Decisions on when to undertake the whole process or part of it depends on the time frame made available for it. For example, one-hour time frames for Sunday school settings would necessitate dividing the process as noted above. The segmented process might also be considered for a series of week night or Saturday sessions, or for periodic partner or family sessions. Weekend retreat settings typically allow for a series of sessions with relatively short break times in between sessions. Therefore, in such settings, each phase of the story-linking process may be engaged singly.

When the intergenerational participants in story-linking are assembled, attention needs to be given to timing the movement through the process. This kind of time management entails paying careful attention to skillful, yet timely, guidance of participants through every step of the process.

Leaders/teachers may aid group processes by stating up front the time frames allotted for each step of the story-linking process. However, in moving through each step, it is important that leaders/teachers are guided by an internal sense of timing. Knowing when to bring closure to group dialogue and reflection and when dialogue should continue is both a gift and a skill that leaders will develop over time.

Being attuned to what we hear, see, and feel as leaders/teachers during the group's activities will guide our sense of timing. For example, being attuned means noticing when spontaneous exuberant dialogue has moved beyond its peak and the time has come to move on. It also means noticing when lengthy dialogue and reflection, even though still intense, must be brought to a close for the sake of moving on to another step and a deeper level of insight and understanding. Such an awareness may prompt the leader/teacher to affirm the group's active participation, indicate the need to move on in the interest of time, and seek the group's agreement to do so. Being attuned may also mean sensing from a participant's expectant or troubled look, forward sitting stance, or half-raised hand that time is needed to encourage and hear her or his response.

In short, knowing the right time to move on to the next step is not an exact science. It is a creative spiritual awareness. It is being in touch with God's moment of bringing meaning to a group or members within it. We call this being in touch with *kairos,* or God's significant moment of acting in our lives.

Reflection Exercise. What decisions about time management would you make in regard to story-linking? On what basis would you decide?

Constructing an Inviting Physical Setting

The arrangement of the physical setting can have a positive or negative effect on group processes. Consequently, attention should be given to it. Of particular importance are such matters as lighting and seating that respond appropriately to the various age groups that will be involved. Moreover, optimal participation occurs when group members are seated in a circle arrangement rather than in theater rows where they cannot have face-to-face contact. Where possible, rooms should also be chosen that allow for movement of chairs into small groups or for role playing and dramatizations.

When using tape recorders to disclose stories in the story-linking process, it is important to assure a volume level that is adequate for the room size and the hearing needs of group members. Materials such as Bibles, newsprint, markers, tape, writing or drawing paper, pencils, pens, crayons, or other desired supplies should be placed on a list and brought in advance of the group's arrival to the meeting room.

Reflection Exercise. Consider a physical setting for undertaking the story-linking process. Where is this setting? What seating and equipment are already there? What arrangements would you need to make in order to create an inviting and comfortable physical setting?

In this chapter, I have introduced approaches to group dynamics and processes in carrying out the story-linking model. My intent has been to suggest approaches to convening groups, mediating groups based on an understanding of developmental stages of groups, tending to group membership and size, time management, and constructing inviting physical settings. The approaches came out of my own experiences. I hope leaders, teachers, and others involved in story-linking will modify them to suit their own specific settings.

SELECTED RESOURCES_ _ _ _ _ _ _ _ _ _

The following selected resources are helpful in preparing for story-linking processes:

Black Americans of Achievement Series. New York: Chelsea House Publishers.

Blacks in the New World Series. Chicago, Ill: University of Illinois Press.

Cone, James H. *The Spirituals and the Blues.* Maryknoll, N.Y.: Orbis Books, 1972.

Crockett, Joseph. *Teaching Scripture from an African American Perspective.* Nashville, Tenn: Discipleship Resources, 1990.

Empak Black History Publications. Empak Publishing Company, 212 E. Ohio Street, Suite 300, Chicago, Ill. 60611.

Evans, Robert A.; Evans, Alice F.; and Weeks, Carolyn. *Casebook for Christian Living: Value Formation for Families and Congregations.* Atlanta: John Knox Press, 1977.

Felder, Cain Hope. *Stony the Road We Trod: African American Biblical Interpretation.* Minneapolis: Fortress Press, 1991.

Hicks, H. Beecher, Jr. *Preaching Through the Storm.* Grand Rapids, Mich.: Ministry Resources, 1987.

Mitchell, Ella Pearson. Editor. *Those Preachin' Women.* Volumes 1 and 2. Valley Forge, Penn.: Judson Press, 1985, 1988.

Philpot, William M. *Best Black Sermons.* Valley Forge, Penn.: Judson Press, 1989.

Proctor, Samuel , and Watley, William. *Sermons from the Black Pulpit.* Valley Forge, Penn.: Judson Press, 1984.

Smith, Jessie Carney, editor. *Notable Black Women.* Detroit: Gale Research, Inc., 1992.

Smith, Judy Gattis. *26 Ways to Use Drama in Teaching the Bible.* Nashville, Tenn.: Abingdon Press, 1988.

Songs of Zion: Supplemental Worship Resources 12. Nashville, Tenn.: Abingdon Press, 1981.

NOTES ___ _

1. A Story-Linking Process

1. See Thomas Dubay, *Caring: A Biblical Theology of Community* (Denville, N.J.: Dimension Books, 1973), pp. 56-57.

2. Exploring Self and World Through Story-Linking

1. See Dorothee Soelle, *Death By Bread Alone: Texts and Reflections on Religious Experience* (Philadelphia: Fortress Press, 1978), pp. 121-123; and Walter Brueggemann, *The Message of the Psalms* (Minneapolis: Augsburg, 1984), p. 26.
2. See Dorothee Soelle, *Death By Bread Alone*, p. 122.
3. Howard Thurman, *Jesus and the Disinherited* (Richmond, Ind.: Friends United Press, 1981), p. 50.
4. The spiritual is found in *Songs of Zion: Supplemental Worship Resources 12* (Nashville: Abingdon Press, 1981), no. 132.

3. Exploring Events of Our Lives Through Story-Linking

1. The story here is excerpted and largely paraphrased from: Josiah Henson, *Father Henson's Story of His Own Life* (Boston: John P. Jewett and Company, 1858).
2. See: Jessie Carney Smith, ed., "Irene McCoy Gaines," *Notable Black American Women* (Detroit: Gale Research, Inc., 1992), pp. 383-86.
3. See: H. Beecher Hicks, Jr., *Preaching Through the Storm* (Grand Rapids: Ministry Resources, 1987), pp. 21-34.

4. Exploring Life Meanings Through Story-Linking

1. The first-person depictions are built on information appearing in Paul J. Achtemeier, *Harper's Bible Dictionary* (San Francisco: Harper & Row, 1985).
2. Frederick Douglass, *Narrative of the Life of Frederick Douglass, An American Slave* (New York: Signet Books, 1968), pp. 76-77.
3. Ibid., p. 83.

4. Ibid., p. 111.
5. Sarah Bradford, *Harriet Tubman: The Moses of Her People* (New York: Corinth, 1961), p. 31.
6. M. W. Taylor, *Harriet Tubman* (New York: Chelsea House, 1991), p. 39.
7. Ibid., p. 73.
8. Ibid., pp. 50-51.
9. The spiritual is found in James Weldon Johnson and J. Rosamund Johnson, *The Books of American Negro Spirituals: The Second Book of Negro Spirituals* (New York: The Viking Press, 1964), p. 180.
10. The spiritual is found in *Songs of Zion: Supplemental Worship Resources 12* (Nashville: Abingdon Press, 1981), no. 123.
11. Langston Hughes, "Mother to Son," in *Children of Promise: African-American Literature and Art for Young People,* ed. Charles Sullivan (New York: Harry N. Abrams, 1991), p. 67.

5. The Pivotal Role of Scripture in Story-Linking and How to Choose Scripture

1. A traditional version and a contemporary arrangement of the spiritual are found in: *Songs of Zion: Supplemental Worship Resources 12* (Nashville: Abingdon Press, 1981), nos. 112 and 212.
2. See: William M. Philpot, ed., *Best Black Sermons* (Valley Forge: Judson Press, 1972), pp. 25-30.
3. The spiritual is found in *Songs of Zion,* no. 106.
4. The spiritual is found in *Songs of Zion,* no. 94.
5. Samuel D. Proctor and William D. Watley, *Sermons From the Black Pulpit* (Valley Forge: Judson Press, 1984), pp. 107-13.
6. Sojourner Truth tells of her mother's frequent use of the language of the Psalmist. See Margaret Washington, ed. *Narrative of Sojourner Truth* (New York: Vintage Books, 1933), p. 7.
7. This was a phrase that Josiah Henson heard his mother cry out on an occasion when her children were sold away from her one by one. See: Josiah Henson, *Father Henson's Story of His Own Life* (Boston: John P. Jewett and Company, 1858), pp. 12-13.
8. *Songs of Zion,* no. 123.
9. This hymn is found in *Songs of Zion,* no. 14.
10. The spiritual is found in *Songs of Zion,* p. 85.
11. The spiritual is found in James Weldon Johnson and J. Rosamund Johnson, *The Books of American Negro Spirituals,* vol. 2 (New York: The Viking Press, 1964), pp. 180-82.
12. This sermon can be found in Samuel D. Proctor and William D. Watley, *Sermons from the Black Pulpit* (Valley Forge: Judson Press, 1984), pp. 99-106.
13. See James Weldon Johnson and J. Rosamund Johnson, *The Books of American Negro Spirituals,* vol. 1, pp. 96-98.
14. The song is found in *Songs of Zion,* no. 132.
15. See John Lovell, Jr., *Black Song: The Forge and the Flame* (New York: Macmillan, 1971), p. 227.
16. Words to the entire gospel song by Thomas Dorsey are found in *Songs of Zion,* no. 189.
17. See John Lovell, Jr., *Black Song: The Forge and the Flame,* p. 231.
18. A gospel song written by George D. Elderkin. See *The New Baptist Hymnal,* 6th ed. (Nashville: National Baptist Publishing Board, 1980), no. 514.

19. *Songs of Zion,* no. 33.
20. James Weldon and J. Rosamund Johnson, *The Books of American Negro Spirituals,* vol. 2, pp. 155-57.
21. James Weldon and J. Rosamund Johnson, *The Books of American Negro Spirituals,* vol. 1, pp. 108-9.
22. These words were taught to me as a young girl by my mother.
23. *Songs of Zion,* no. 126.
24. Ibid., no. 88
25. Ibid., no. 235.
26. See Walter H. Brooks, *The Pastor's Voice* (Washington, D.C.: Associated Publishers, 1945), p. 113.
27. *Songs of Zion,* no. 76.
28. *The Books of American Negro Spirituals,* vol. 2, p. 180.
29. Ibid., pp. 130-33.
30. These words to the spiritual were sung in the community of my childhood. A variation appears in John Lovell, Jr., *Black Song: The Forge and the Flame,* p. 323.
31. For further description and history of the Common Lectionary, see William H. Willimon, "Lectionary," pp. 371-72 in *Harper's Encyclopedia of Religious Education,* ed., Iris V. Cully and Kendig Brubaker Cully (New York: Harper & Row, 1990); Hoyt Hickman, Don Saliers, Laurence Hull Stookey, and James F. White, *The New Handbook of the Christian Year* (Nashville: Abingdon Press, 1991).
32. For the precise method presented by Hessel, see Dieter T. Hessel, "Developing a Whole Parish Praxis," pp. 269-72 in *Social Themes of the Christian Year* (Louisville: Westminster/John Knox, 1983). The seven points can be found on pp. 270-72.
33. For additional information on the uniform lesson series, see: A. O. Van Eck, "Uniform Lessons Series," pp. 669-70 in *Harper's Encyclopedia of Religious Education.*